Math Practice: Grades 4–5

Table of Contents

ISBN 978-1-60418-271-2
04-248121151

Ready-to-Use Ideas and Activities

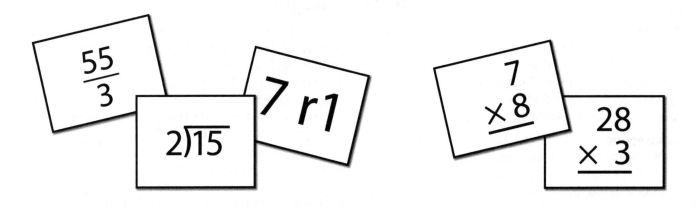

The only way that students will truly be able to manipulate numbers and have access to higher-level math concepts is to learn the basic facts and understand fundamental concepts, such as counting, addition, subtraction, multiplication, and division.

The following activities can help reinforce basic skills. These activities include a multisensory approach to helping students understand the concepts being introduced.

- Separate the flash cards provided in the back of this book. Place the "equal" sign, "greater than" sign, and "lesser than" sign flash cards on a flat surface. Then, place two flash cards with equations on the flat surface. Have student use the sign flash cards to show whether the two equations are equal, one equation is greater than the other equation, or one equation is less than the other equation. Repeat with two different equation flash cards.

Multiplying One- and Two-Digit Numbers

Solve each problem. Regroup when necessary.

1. 48
   × 9

2. 28
   × 3

3. 54
   × 8

4. 82
   × 6

5. 12
   × 7

6. 53
   × 5

7. 27
   × 4

8. 56
   × 2

9. 37
   × 5

10. 77
    × 7

11. 57
    × 4

12. 34
    × 9

13. 85
    × 3

14. 82
    × 7

15. 16
    × 4

16. 53
    × 8

17. 14
    × 9

18. 46
    × 5

19. 72
    × 8

20. 69
    × 3

21. 26
    × 5

22. 62
    × 5

23. 43
    × 4

24. 78
    × 6

25. 35
    × 6

26. 34
    × 3

27. 39
    × 7

28. 43
    × 6

29. 25
    × 2

30. 26
    × 7

Multiplying One- and Three-Digit Numbers

Solve each problem. Regroup when necessary.

1. 323
   × 5

2. 515
   × 4

3. 255
   × 4

4. 915
   × 2

5. 860
   × 2

6. 561
   × 9

7. 109
   × 4

8. 812
   × 8

9. 503
   × 3

10. 827
    × 3

11. 122
    × 8

12. 523
    × 6

13. 206
    × 5

14. 617
    × 7

15. 134
    × 6

16. 905
    × 5

17. 706
    × 4

18. 422
    × 5

19. 423
    × 6

20. 415
    × 2

21. 584
    × 3

22. 234
    × 5

23. 342
    × 5

24. 256
    × 5

25. 816
    × 2

26. 715
    × 7

27. 804
    × 6

28. 316
    × 7

29. 715
    × 4

30. 121
    × 9

Name _____   Date _____

Multiplying One- and Four-Digit Numbers

Solve each problem. Regroup when necessary.

1. $2,582 \times 7$

2. $3,251 \times 4$

3. $1,067 \times 3$

4. $3,610 \times 4$

5. $7,564 \times 5$

6. $5,831 \times 4$

7. $4,108 \times 2$

8. $7,109 \times 8$

9. $2,000 \times 6$

10. $2,168 \times 6$

11. $6,528 \times 9$

12. $5,672 \times 3$

13. $5,306 \times 3$

14. $6,241 \times 7$

15. $6,384 \times 9$

16. $4,634 \times 2$

17. $8,436 \times 5$

18. $5,691 \times 5$

19. $1,029 \times 5$

20. $5,414 \times 2$

21. $6,501 \times 7$

22. $2,897 \times 4$

23. $7,152 \times 4$

24. $4,646 \times 9$

25. $5,678 \times 2$

26. $4,610 \times 5$

27. $5,129 \times 5$

28. $3,162 \times 4$

29. $7,109 \times 6$

30. $4,862 \times 7$

Multiplying Two-Digit Numbers

Solve each problem. Regroup when necessary.

1. $\begin{array}{r} 41 \\ \times\,18 \\ \hline \end{array}$
2. $\begin{array}{r} 53 \\ \times\,38 \\ \hline \end{array}$
3. $\begin{array}{r} 73 \\ \times\,46 \\ \hline \end{array}$
4. $\begin{array}{r} 42 \\ \times\,30 \\ \hline \end{array}$
5. $\begin{array}{r} 86 \\ \times\,75 \\ \hline \end{array}$

6. $\begin{array}{r} 38 \\ \times\,22 \\ \hline \end{array}$
7. $\begin{array}{r} 36 \\ \times\,12 \\ \hline \end{array}$
8. $\begin{array}{r} 62 \\ \times\,44 \\ \hline \end{array}$
9. $\begin{array}{r} 81 \\ \times\,72 \\ \hline \end{array}$
10. $\begin{array}{r} 56 \\ \times\,13 \\ \hline \end{array}$

11. $\begin{array}{r} 64 \\ \times\,47 \\ \hline \end{array}$
12. $\begin{array}{r} 82 \\ \times\,51 \\ \hline \end{array}$
13. $\begin{array}{r} 25 \\ \times\,17 \\ \hline \end{array}$
14. $\begin{array}{r} 91 \\ \times\,43 \\ \hline \end{array}$
15. $\begin{array}{r} 49 \\ \times\,28 \\ \hline \end{array}$

16. $\begin{array}{r} 68 \\ \times\,32 \\ \hline \end{array}$
17. $\begin{array}{r} 42 \\ \times\,18 \\ \hline \end{array}$
18. $\begin{array}{r} 86 \\ \times\,42 \\ \hline \end{array}$
19. $\begin{array}{r} 35 \\ \times\,28 \\ \hline \end{array}$
20. $\begin{array}{r} 73 \\ \times\,56 \\ \hline \end{array}$

21. $\begin{array}{r} 72 \\ \times\,43 \\ \hline \end{array}$
22. $\begin{array}{r} 58 \\ \times\,63 \\ \hline \end{array}$
23. $\begin{array}{r} 83 \\ \times\,27 \\ \hline \end{array}$
24. $\begin{array}{r} 70 \\ \times\,60 \\ \hline \end{array}$
25. $\begin{array}{r} 54 \\ \times\,27 \\ \hline \end{array}$

Multiplying Two- and Three-Digit Numbers

Solve each problem. Regroup when necessary.

1. $\begin{array}{r} 518 \\ \times\ 42 \\ \hline \end{array}$

2. $\begin{array}{r} 216 \\ \times\ 10 \\ \hline \end{array}$

3. $\begin{array}{r} 443 \\ \times\ 33 \\ \hline \end{array}$

4. $\begin{array}{r} 687 \\ \times\ 51 \\ \hline \end{array}$

5. $\begin{array}{r} 554 \\ \times\ 53 \\ \hline \end{array}$

6. $\begin{array}{r} 729 \\ \times\ 56 \\ \hline \end{array}$

7. $\begin{array}{r} 591 \\ \times\ 19 \\ \hline \end{array}$

8. $\begin{array}{r} 248 \\ \times\ 75 \\ \hline \end{array}$

9. $\begin{array}{r} 792 \\ \times\ 43 \\ \hline \end{array}$

10. $\begin{array}{r} 456 \\ \times\ 14 \\ \hline \end{array}$

11. $\begin{array}{r} 455 \\ \times\ 31 \\ \hline \end{array}$

12. $\begin{array}{r} 327 \\ \times\ 35 \\ \hline \end{array}$

13. $\begin{array}{r} 697 \\ \times\ 46 \\ \hline \end{array}$

14. $\begin{array}{r} 826 \\ \times\ 26 \\ \hline \end{array}$

15. $\begin{array}{r} 647 \\ \times\ 18 \\ \hline \end{array}$

16. $\begin{array}{r} 512 \\ \times\ 60 \\ \hline \end{array}$

17. $\begin{array}{r} 244 \\ \times\ 32 \\ \hline \end{array}$

18. $\begin{array}{r} 843 \\ \times\ 12 \\ \hline \end{array}$

19. $\begin{array}{r} 746 \\ \times\ 37 \\ \hline \end{array}$

20. $\begin{array}{r} 535 \\ \times\ 79 \\ \hline \end{array}$

21. $\begin{array}{r} 485 \\ \times\ 21 \\ \hline \end{array}$

22. $\begin{array}{r} 123 \\ \times\ 45 \\ \hline \end{array}$

23. $\begin{array}{r} 695 \\ \times\ 61 \\ \hline \end{array}$

24. $\begin{array}{r} 792 \\ \times\ 49 \\ \hline \end{array}$

25. $\begin{array}{r} 691 \\ \times\ 24 \\ \hline \end{array}$

Multiplying Three-Digit Numbers

Total Problems:	**30**
Problems Correct:	_____

Solve each problem. Regroup when necessary.

1. 654
    × 189

2. 542
    × 172

3. 323
    × 247

4. 826
    × 825

5. 340
    × 285

6. 221
    × 103

7. 365
    × 184

8. 756
    × 633

9. 236
    × 420

10. 630
    × 246

11. 416
    × 122

12. 593
    × 347

13. 724
    × 377

14. 351
    × 240

15. 577
    × 290

16. 412
    × 203

17. 593
    × 347

18. 724
    × 377

19. 251
    × 141

20. 472
    × 184

21. 350
    × 491

22. 827
    × 579

23. 520
    × 397

24. 630
    × 141

25. 770
    × 143

26. 321
    × 324

27. 427
    × 273

28. 678
    × 459

29. 517
    × 510

30. 370
    × 237

Division with One-Digit Quotients

Total Problems: **27**
Problems Correct: _____

Solve each problem.

1. $3\overline{)12}$

2. $4\overline{)12}$

3. $8\overline{)48}$

4. $4\overline{)24}$

5. $5\overline{)15}$

6. $9\overline{)72}$

7. $5\overline{)10}$

8. $6\overline{)42}$

9. $7\overline{)42}$

10. $3\overline{)9}$

11. $6\overline{)54}$

12. $4\overline{)28}$

13. $2\overline{)8}$

14. $7\overline{)63}$

15. $8\overline{)56}$

16. $30 \div 5 =$

17. $35 \div 7 =$

18. $14 \div 7 =$

19. $36 \div 9 =$

20. $12 \div 6 =$

21. $21 \div 7 =$

22. $24 \div 6 =$

23. $64 \div 8 =$

24. $36 \div 9 =$

25. $32 \div 4 =$

26. $20 \div 5 =$

27. $18 \div 6 =$

Division with Two-Digit Quotients

Total Problems: **30**
Problems Correct: _____

Solve each problem.

1. $6\overline{)72}$ **2.** $5\overline{)90}$ **3.** $3\overline{)93}$

4. $2\overline{)36}$ **5.** $3\overline{)96}$ **6.** $3\overline{)66}$

7. $7\overline{)98}$ **8.** $4\overline{)72}$ **9.** $7\overline{)91}$

10. $4\overline{)40}$ **11.** $7\overline{)84}$ **12.** $6\overline{)78}$

13. $3\overline{)36}$ **14.** $7\overline{)70}$ **15.** $8\overline{)88}$

16. $5\overline{)55}$ **17.** $5\overline{)90}$ **18.** $5\overline{)95}$

19. $2\overline{)24}$ **20.** $6\overline{)84}$ **21.** $9\overline{)99}$

22. $3\overline{)81}$ **23.** $3\overline{)75}$ **24.** $3\overline{)51}$

25. $8\overline{)80}$ **26.** $2\overline{)86}$ **27.** $4\overline{)96}$

28. $3\overline{)45}$ **29.** $5\overline{)85}$ **30.** $8\overline{)80}$

 CD-104321 • © Carson-Dellosa

Division with Three-Digit Quotients

Solve each problem.

1. $9\overline{)1,368}$

2. $4\overline{)1,228}$

3. $8\overline{)5,392}$

4. $6\overline{)1,878}$

5. $5\overline{)1,395}$

6. $7\overline{)2,926}$

7. $4\overline{)1,008}$

8. $5\overline{)975}$

9. $4\overline{)2,128}$

10. $2\overline{)1,224}$

11. $6\overline{)2,706}$

12. $3\overline{)2,019}$

13. $3\overline{)1,008}$

14. $8\overline{)3,888}$

15. $7\overline{)1,421}$

16. $5\overline{)1,125}$

17. $2\overline{)1,024}$

18. $3\overline{)1,134}$

19. $8\overline{)4,960}$

20. $9\overline{)2,790}$

Division with One- and Two-Digit Quotients and Remainders

Solve each problem.

1. $7\overline{)82}$

2. $4\overline{)54}$

3. $3\overline{)26}$

4. $8\overline{)95}$

5. $4\overline{)18}$

6. $7\overline{)57}$

7. $4\overline{)63}$

8. $5\overline{)22}$

9. $5\overline{)18}$

10. $5\overline{)81}$

11. $4\overline{)41}$

12. $3\overline{)29}$

13. $6\overline{)74}$

14. $8\overline{)37}$

15. $5\overline{)42}$

16. $23 \div 5 =$

17. $58 \div 7 =$

18. $46 \div 5 =$

19. $24 \div 7 =$

20. $45 \div 6 =$

21. $51 \div 7 =$

22. $32 \div 6 =$

23. $26 \div 3 =$

24. $25 \div 4 =$

25. $43 \div 2 =$

26. $19 \div 2 =$

27. $87 \div 9 =$

Division with Two-Digit Quotients and Remainders

Solve each problem.

1. $6\overline{)82}$

2. $2\overline{)39}$

3. $8\overline{)89}$

4. $4\overline{)85}$

5. $4\overline{)70}$

6. $7\overline{)93}$

7. $3\overline{)59}$

8. $6\overline{)82}$

9. $2\overline{)81}$

10. $2\overline{)23}$

11. $8\overline{)94}$

12. $5\overline{)82}$

13. $4\overline{)97}$

14. $8\overline{)97}$

15. $7\overline{)92}$

16. $7\overline{)79}$

17. $5\overline{)79}$

18. $6\overline{)89}$

19. $5\overline{)63}$

20. $6\overline{)83}$

21. $7\overline{)81}$

22. $6\overline{)85}$

23. $6\overline{)89}$

24. $9\overline{)98}$

25. $3\overline{)67}$

26. $5\overline{)63}$

27. $6\overline{)73}$

28. $3\overline{)83}$

29. $7\overline{)85}$

30. $3\overline{)47}$

Name _____   Date _____

Division with Three-Digit Quotients and Remainders

Total Problems: **20**
Problems Correct: _____

Solve each problem.

1. 4)873

2. 5)943

3. 8)957

4. 9)987

5. 7)915

6. 5)527

7. 2)597

8. 9)973

9. 4)574

10. 6)653

11. 3)784

12. 4)486

13. 3)629

14. 2)301

15. 5)637

16. 4)862

17. 2)733

18. 8)937

19. 3)574

20. 4)653

Name _____ Date _____

Division with Two-Digit Divisors

Total Problems: **20**
Problems Correct: _____

Solve each problem.

1. 32)512

2. 52)624

3. 18)450

4. 32)768

5. 62)992

6. 41)820

7. 12)144

8. 32)960

9. 18)702

10. 39)858

11. 15)540

12. 23)345

13. 56)952

14. 47)517

15. 27)810

16. 26)338

17. 25)350

18. 45)990

19. 24)600

20. 54)864

Division with Two-Digit Divisors and Remainders

Solve each problem.

1. $67\overline{)807}$ **2.** $37\overline{)369}$ **3.** $64\overline{)654}$ **4.** $81\overline{)921}$

5. $61\overline{)741}$ **6.** $58\overline{)368}$ **7.** $18\overline{)652}$ **8.** $23\overline{)875}$

9. $13\overline{)235}$ **10.** $40\overline{)142}$ **11.** $25\overline{)465}$ **12.** $11\overline{)505}$

13. $19\overline{)410}$ **14.** $32\overline{)458}$ **15.** $53\overline{)367}$ **16.** $45\overline{)787}$

17. $22\overline{)268}$ **18.** $42\overline{)632}$ **19.** $56\overline{)647}$ **20.** $87\overline{)357}$

Name _____ Date _____

Division with Two-Digit Divisors and Remainders

Solve each problem.

1. 43)‾1,256‾

2. 48)‾2,541‾

3. 65)‾1,596‾

4. 22)‾7,321‾

5. 21)‾3,010‾

6. 39)‾8,563‾

7. 82)‾4,512‾

8. 37)‾2,148‾

9. 30)‾6,172‾

10. 78)‾5,000‾

11. 77)‾2,159‾

12. 85)‾3,578‾

13. 59)‾8,787‾

14. 55)‾9,999‾

15. 27)‾3,265‾

16. 56)‾5,892‾

Learning About Fractions

Shade each shape to show the correct fraction.

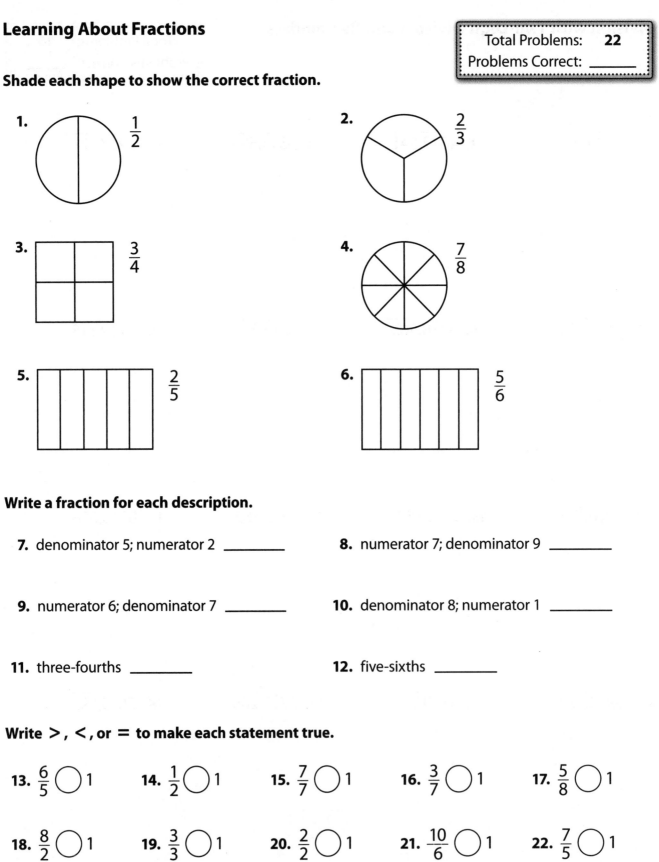

1. $\frac{1}{2}$

2. $\frac{2}{3}$

3. $\frac{3}{4}$

4. $\frac{7}{8}$

5. $\frac{2}{5}$

6. $\frac{5}{6}$

Write a fraction for each description.

7. denominator 5; numerator 2 _____

8. numerator 7; denominator 9 _____

9. numerator 6; denominator 7 _____

10. denominator 8; numerator 1 _____

11. three-fourths _____

12. five-sixths _____

Write > , < , or = to make each statement true.

13. $\frac{6}{5}$ ◯ 1

14. $\frac{1}{2}$ ◯ 1

15. $\frac{7}{7}$ ◯ 1

16. $\frac{3}{7}$ ◯ 1

17. $\frac{5}{8}$ ◯ 1

18. $\frac{8}{2}$ ◯ 1

19. $\frac{3}{3}$ ◯ 1

20. $\frac{2}{2}$ ◯ 1

21. $\frac{10}{6}$ ◯ 1

22. $\frac{7}{5}$ ◯ 1

Reducing Fractions

Write each fraction in simplest form.

1. $\frac{6}{8}$ =

2. $\frac{3}{24}$ =

3. $\frac{20}{35}$ =

4. $\frac{15}{20}$ =

5. $\frac{10}{20}$ =

6. $\frac{6}{16}$ =

7. $\frac{5}{20}$ =

8. $\frac{4}{8}$ =

9. $\frac{4}{16}$ =

10. $\frac{6}{9}$ =

11. $\frac{4}{20}$ =

12. $\frac{3}{15}$ =

13. $\frac{3}{12}$ =

14. $\frac{5}{15}$ =

15. $\frac{8}{16}$ =

16. $\frac{7}{21}$ =

17. $\frac{5}{25}$ =

18. $\frac{15}{30}$ =

19. $\frac{2}{8}$ =

20. $\frac{14}{21}$ =

21. $\frac{12}{16}$ =

22. $\frac{16}{32}$ =

23. $\frac{7}{35}$ =

24. $\frac{20}{40}$ =

25. $\frac{17}{34}$ =

26. $\frac{10}{12}$ =

27. $\frac{16}{24}$ =

28. $\frac{6}{18}$ =

29. $\frac{5}{10}$ =

30. $\frac{24}{32}$ =

Reducing Fractions

Write each fraction in simplest form.

1. $\dfrac{4}{8} =$ 2. $\dfrac{7}{14} =$ 3. $\dfrac{20}{30} =$

4. $\dfrac{10}{28} =$ 5. $\dfrac{14}{40} =$ 6. $\dfrac{6}{20} =$

7. $\dfrac{4}{12} =$ 8. $\dfrac{2}{8} =$ 9. $\dfrac{5}{30} =$

10. $\dfrac{3}{9} =$ 11. $\dfrac{2}{6} =$ 12. $\dfrac{3}{15} =$

13. $\dfrac{3}{12} =$ 14. $\dfrac{8}{24} =$ 15. $\dfrac{8}{20} =$

16. $\dfrac{6}{18} =$ 17. $\dfrac{5}{20} =$ 18. $\dfrac{15}{20} =$

19. $\dfrac{2}{4} =$ 20. $\dfrac{15}{21} =$ 21. $\dfrac{12}{30} =$

22. $\dfrac{20}{22} =$ 23. $\dfrac{7}{28} =$ 24. $\dfrac{16}{32} =$

25. $\dfrac{12}{15} =$ 26. $\dfrac{18}{24} =$ 27. $\dfrac{4}{18} =$

28. $\dfrac{5}{15} =$ 29. $\dfrac{15}{20} =$ 30. $\dfrac{21}{45} =$

Comparing Fractions

Total Problems: **21**
Problems Correct: _____

Write **>** , **<** , or **=** to make each statement true.

1. $\frac{16}{52}$ ◯ $\frac{16}{25}$

2. $\frac{13}{21}$ ◯ $\frac{10}{13}$

3. $\frac{16}{20}$ ◯ $\frac{10}{25}$

4. $\frac{12}{32}$ ◯ $\frac{12}{24}$

5. $\frac{14}{16}$ ◯ $\frac{15}{20}$

6. $\frac{56}{88}$ ◯ $\frac{25}{55}$

7. $\frac{16}{16}$ ◯ $\frac{25}{25}$

8. $\frac{4}{5}$ ◯ $\frac{5}{6}$

9. $\frac{9}{10}$ ◯ $\frac{8}{15}$

10. $\frac{12}{24}$ ◯ $\frac{2}{4}$

11. $\frac{9}{15}$ ◯ $\frac{4}{10}$

12. $\frac{6}{15}$ ◯ $\frac{4}{20}$

13. $\frac{16}{36}$ ◯ $\frac{24}{27}$

14. $\frac{25}{30}$ ◯ $\frac{3}{18}$

15. $\frac{7}{8}$ ◯ $\frac{5}{9}$

16. $\frac{1}{2}$ ◯ $\frac{24}{50}$

17. $\frac{18}{21}$ ◯ $\frac{12}{28}$

18. $\frac{9}{12}$ ◯ $\frac{15}{20}$

19. $\frac{35}{39}$ ◯ $\frac{14}{24}$

20. $\frac{16}{24}$ ◯ $\frac{20}{30}$

21. $\frac{21}{35}$ ◯ $\frac{16}{24}$

Writing Improper Fractions as Mixed Numbers

Write each improper fraction as a mixed number in simplest form.

1. $\dfrac{4}{3} =$

2. $\dfrac{20}{15} =$

3. $\dfrac{7}{4} =$

4. $\dfrac{55}{12} =$

5. $\dfrac{18}{5} =$

6. $\dfrac{5}{2} =$

7. $\dfrac{5}{3} =$

8. $\dfrac{12}{5} =$

9. $\dfrac{13}{4} =$

10. $\dfrac{15}{6} =$

11. $\dfrac{13}{2} =$

12. $\dfrac{17}{9} =$

13. $\dfrac{10}{4} =$

14. $\dfrac{19}{2} =$

15. $\dfrac{27}{5} =$

16. $\dfrac{15}{4} =$

17. $\dfrac{8}{3} =$

18. $\dfrac{15}{8} =$

19. $\dfrac{6}{4} =$

20. $\dfrac{43}{7} =$

21. $\dfrac{19}{11} =$

22. $\dfrac{20}{7} =$

23. $\dfrac{9}{4} =$

24. $\dfrac{17}{4} =$

25. $\dfrac{10}{3} =$

26. $\dfrac{24}{10} =$

27. $\dfrac{9}{8} =$

28. $\dfrac{16}{3} =$

29. $\dfrac{10}{3} =$

30. $\dfrac{50}{6} =$

Name _____ Date _____

Writing Improper Fractions as Mixed Numbers

Write each improper fraction as a mixed number in simplest form.

Total Problems: **30**
Problems Correct: _____

1. $\dfrac{6}{4} =$

2. $\dfrac{21}{12} =$

3. $\dfrac{9}{4} =$

4. $\dfrac{25}{11} =$

5. $\dfrac{19}{5} =$

6. $\dfrac{3}{2} =$

7. $\dfrac{7}{4} =$

8. $\dfrac{13}{3} =$

9. $\dfrac{14}{6} =$

10. $\dfrac{16}{5} =$

11. $\dfrac{13}{5} =$

12. $\dfrac{14}{8} =$

13. $\dfrac{11}{2} =$

14. $\dfrac{17}{4} =$

15. $\dfrac{19}{2} =$

16. $\dfrac{25}{3} =$

17. $\dfrac{8}{3} =$

18. $\dfrac{11}{6} =$

19. $\dfrac{10}{3} =$

20. $\dfrac{33}{6} =$

21. $\dfrac{14}{9} =$

22. $\dfrac{21}{8} =$

23. $\dfrac{7}{4} =$

24. $\dfrac{13}{3} =$

25. $\dfrac{12}{5} =$

26. $\dfrac{18}{11} =$

27. $\dfrac{9}{2} =$

28. $\dfrac{15}{4} =$

29. $\dfrac{10}{6} =$

30. $\dfrac{10}{4} =$

Name _____ Date _____

Writing Improper Fractions as Mixed Numbers

Total Problems: **30**
Problems Correct: _____

Write each improper fraction as a mixed number in simplest form.

1. $\frac{9}{2} =$

2. $\frac{51}{10} =$

3. $\frac{19}{5} =$

4. $\frac{8}{7} =$

5. $\frac{14}{13} =$

6. $\frac{8}{5} =$

7. $\frac{12}{5} =$

8. $\frac{13}{7} =$

9. $\frac{16}{9} =$

10. $\frac{10}{6} =$

11. $\frac{17}{7} =$

12. $\frac{13}{11} =$

13. $\frac{11}{2} =$

14. $\frac{17}{6} =$

15. $\frac{25}{8} =$

16. $\frac{11}{10} =$

17. $\frac{19}{18} =$

18. $\frac{26}{22} =$

19. $\frac{16}{3} =$

20. $\frac{12}{5} =$

21. $\frac{3}{2} =$

22. $\frac{61}{3} =$

23. $\frac{13}{12} =$

24. $\frac{47}{13} =$

25. $\frac{11}{5} =$

26. $\frac{15}{14} =$

27. $\frac{6}{5} =$

28. $\frac{15}{13} =$

29. $\frac{19}{11} =$

30. $\frac{10}{9} =$

Writing Improper Fractions as Mixed Numbers

Write each improper fraction as a mixed number in simplest form.

1. $\frac{23}{15} =$

2. $\frac{40}{24} =$

3. $\frac{97}{33} =$

4. $\frac{55}{12} =$

5. $\frac{26}{12} =$

6. $\frac{36}{34} =$

7. $\frac{32}{15} =$

8. $\frac{89}{17} =$

9. $\frac{26}{15} =$

10. $\frac{13}{4} =$

11. $\frac{59}{25} =$

12. $\frac{10}{8} =$

13. $\frac{48}{5} =$

14. $\frac{66}{50} =$

15. $\frac{13}{3} =$

16. $\frac{15}{4} =$

17. $\frac{6}{4} =$

18. $\frac{64}{49} =$

19. $\frac{26}{4} =$

20. $\frac{44}{16} =$

21. $\frac{24}{20} =$

22. $\frac{20}{7} =$

23. $\frac{17}{6} =$

24. $\frac{56}{11} =$

25. $\frac{29}{7} =$

26. $\frac{62}{9} =$

27. $\frac{8}{3} =$

28. $\frac{16}{3} =$

29. $\frac{20}{8} =$

30. $\frac{35}{12} =$

Writing Mixed Numbers as Improper Fractions

Write each mixed number as an improper fraction.

1. $3\frac{1}{2} =$

2. $5\frac{7}{8} =$

3. $7\frac{4}{5} =$

4. $1\frac{1}{10} =$

5. $6\frac{5}{8} =$

6. $5\frac{2}{3} =$

7. $9\frac{1}{2} =$

8. $4\frac{3}{8} =$

9. $8\frac{2}{3} =$

10. $2\frac{2}{3} =$

11. $2\frac{4}{9} =$

12. $4\frac{3}{4} =$

13. $2\frac{3}{8} =$

14. $4\frac{2}{4} =$

15. $6\frac{5}{7} =$

16. $10\frac{3}{5} =$

17. $4\frac{5}{9} =$

18. $12\frac{13}{15} =$

19. $3\frac{1}{3} =$

20. $4\frac{2}{3} =$

21. $6\frac{1}{5} =$

Writing Mixed Numbers as Improper Fractions

Write each mixed number as an improper fraction.

1. $1\frac{2}{3} =$ 　　　　　　　**2.** $10\frac{5}{6} =$ 　　　　　　**3.** $5\frac{4}{5} =$

4. $2\frac{1}{12} =$ 　　　　　　**5.** $12\frac{4}{5} =$ 　　　　　　**6.** $1\frac{1}{5} =$

7. $7\frac{1}{6} =$ 　　　　　　　**8.** $9\frac{6}{8} =$ 　　　　　　**9.** $9\frac{2}{8} =$

10. $20\frac{2}{8} =$ 　　　　　　**11.** $8\frac{3}{9} =$ 　　　　　　**12.** $3\frac{3}{8} =$

13. $2\frac{3}{4} =$ 　　　　　　**14.** $1\frac{1}{4} =$ 　　　　　　**15.** $15\frac{3}{4} =$

16. $7\frac{10}{16} =$ 　　　　　**17.** $11\frac{3}{9} =$ 　　　　　**18.** $7\frac{5}{6} =$

19. $3\frac{2}{5} =$ 　　　　　　**20.** $6\frac{1}{3} =$ 　　　　　　**21.** $7\frac{2}{5} =$

Name _____ Date _____

Making Fractions Equivalent

Total Problems: **24**
Problems Correct: _____

Write the missing numerator to make each pair equivalent.

1. $\dfrac{2}{3} = \dfrac{}{12}$

2. $\dfrac{8}{9} = \dfrac{}{54}$

3. $\dfrac{1}{2} = \dfrac{}{10}$

4. $\dfrac{1}{8} = \dfrac{}{32}$

5. $\dfrac{4}{9} = \dfrac{}{81}$

6. $\dfrac{2}{9} = \dfrac{}{18}$

7. $\dfrac{3}{4} = \dfrac{}{16}$

8. $\dfrac{1}{2} = \dfrac{}{12}$

9. $\dfrac{4}{5} = \dfrac{}{25}$

10. $\dfrac{2}{5} = \dfrac{}{30}$

11. $\dfrac{7}{8} = \dfrac{}{64}$

12. $\dfrac{2}{3} = \dfrac{}{15}$

13. $\dfrac{2}{5} = \dfrac{}{10}$

14. $\dfrac{3}{8} = \dfrac{}{16}$

15. $\dfrac{5}{8} = \dfrac{}{24}$

16. $\dfrac{3}{4} = \dfrac{}{24}$

17. $\dfrac{3}{5} = \dfrac{}{15}$

18. $\dfrac{3}{7} = \dfrac{}{14}$

19. $\dfrac{1}{6} = \dfrac{}{12}$

20. $\dfrac{4}{5} = \dfrac{}{20}$

21. $\dfrac{3}{7} = \dfrac{}{21}$

22. $\dfrac{5}{6} = \dfrac{}{42}$

23. $\dfrac{1}{6} = \dfrac{}{36}$

24. $\dfrac{5}{8} = \dfrac{}{40}$

Making Fractions Equivalent

Write the missing numerators to make the fractions in each row equivalent.

1. $\dfrac{1}{2} = \dfrac{}{36} = \dfrac{}{18} = \dfrac{}{16} = \dfrac{}{42} = \dfrac{}{48}$

2. $\dfrac{5}{6} = \dfrac{}{48} = \dfrac{}{12} = \dfrac{}{30} = \dfrac{}{18} = \dfrac{}{24}$

3. $\dfrac{1}{3} = \dfrac{}{9} = \dfrac{}{27} = \dfrac{}{90} = \dfrac{}{6} = \dfrac{}{12}$

4. $\dfrac{3}{4} = \dfrac{}{24} = \dfrac{}{16} = \dfrac{}{8} = \dfrac{}{20} = \dfrac{}{36}$

5. $\dfrac{4}{9} = \dfrac{}{18} = \dfrac{}{45} = \dfrac{}{36} = \dfrac{}{54} = \dfrac{}{27}$

6. $\dfrac{7}{8} = \dfrac{}{16} = \dfrac{}{56} = \dfrac{}{24} = \dfrac{}{48} = \dfrac{}{32}$

7. $\dfrac{3}{7} = \dfrac{}{21} = \dfrac{}{42} = \dfrac{}{14} = \dfrac{}{35} = \dfrac{}{28}$

8. $\dfrac{2}{5} = \dfrac{}{50} = \dfrac{}{10} = \dfrac{}{40} = \dfrac{}{15} = \dfrac{}{25}$

Making Fractions Equivalent

Write the missing numerator to make each pair equivalent.

1. $4 = \dfrac{}{3}$

2. $6 = \dfrac{}{5}$

3. $\dfrac{2}{3} = \dfrac{}{18}$

4. $\dfrac{1}{5} = \dfrac{}{20}$

5. $\dfrac{5}{6} = \dfrac{}{48}$

6. $\dfrac{1}{6} = \dfrac{}{36}$

7. $\dfrac{1}{2} = \dfrac{}{8}$

8. $4 = \dfrac{}{2}$

9. $3 = \dfrac{}{2}$

10. $\dfrac{5}{8} = \dfrac{}{40}$

11. $\dfrac{1}{3} = \dfrac{}{36}$

12. $\dfrac{2}{7} = \dfrac{}{49}$

13. $\dfrac{1}{3} = \dfrac{}{6}$

14. $\dfrac{5}{6} = \dfrac{}{24}$

15. $2 = \dfrac{}{4}$

16. $\dfrac{1}{4} = \dfrac{}{16}$

17. $\dfrac{1}{8} = \dfrac{}{64}$

18. $\dfrac{2}{5} = \dfrac{}{30}$

19. $\dfrac{2}{5} = \dfrac{}{10}$

20. $\dfrac{7}{8} = \dfrac{}{64}$

21. $\dfrac{2}{3} = \dfrac{}{15}$

22. $\dfrac{3}{5} = \dfrac{}{15}$

23. $\dfrac{3}{4} = \dfrac{}{24}$

24. $\dfrac{7}{8} = \dfrac{}{56}$

Adding Fractions with Like Denominators

Solve each problem. Write the answer in simplest form.

1. $\dfrac{1}{3} + \dfrac{2}{3} =$

2. $\dfrac{2}{9} + \dfrac{5}{9} =$

3. $\dfrac{1}{6} + \dfrac{1}{6} =$

4. $\dfrac{3}{6} + \dfrac{1}{6} =$

5. $\dfrac{2}{4} + \dfrac{2}{4} =$

6. $\dfrac{1}{2} + \dfrac{1}{2} =$

7. $\dfrac{5}{8} + \dfrac{3}{8} =$

8. $\dfrac{5}{5} + \dfrac{2}{5} =$

9. $\dfrac{2}{10} + \dfrac{4}{10} =$

10. $\dfrac{1}{2} + \dfrac{1}{2} =$

11. $\dfrac{3}{5} + \dfrac{2}{5} =$

12. $\dfrac{3}{7} + \dfrac{2}{7} =$

13. $\dfrac{1}{3} + \dfrac{2}{3} =$

14. $\dfrac{1}{7} + \dfrac{1}{7} =$

15. $\dfrac{1}{6} + \dfrac{4}{6} =$

Adding Fractions with Like Denominators

Solve each problem. Write the answer in simplest form.

1. $\dfrac{2}{7}$
$+\dfrac{3}{7}$

2. $\dfrac{6}{8}$
$+\dfrac{1}{8}$

3. $\dfrac{7}{10}$
$+\dfrac{9}{10}$

4. $\dfrac{3}{7}$
$+\dfrac{1}{7}$

5. $\dfrac{1}{5}$
$+\dfrac{3}{5}$

6. $\dfrac{3}{5}$
$+\dfrac{3}{5}$

7. $\dfrac{1}{4}$
$+\dfrac{2}{4}$

8. $\dfrac{1}{5}$
$+\dfrac{3}{5}$

9. $\dfrac{4}{8}$
$+\dfrac{2}{8}$

10. $\dfrac{6}{7}$
$+\dfrac{5}{7}$

11. $\dfrac{1}{8}$
$+\dfrac{5}{8}$

12. $\dfrac{2}{8}$
$+\dfrac{4}{8}$

13. $\dfrac{2}{10}$
$+\dfrac{4}{10}$

14. $\dfrac{3}{4}$
$+\dfrac{2}{4}$

15. $\dfrac{2}{3}$
$+\dfrac{1}{3}$

16. $\dfrac{4}{9}$
$+\dfrac{3}{9}$

17. $\dfrac{2}{6}$
$+\dfrac{1}{6}$

18. $\dfrac{5}{12}$
$+\dfrac{5}{12}$

19. $\dfrac{1}{6}$
$+\dfrac{3}{6}$

20. $\dfrac{2}{9}$
$+\dfrac{1}{9}$

Adding Mixed Numbers with Like Denominators

Solve each problem. Write the answer in simplest form.

Total Problems: **12**
Problems Correct: _____

1. $2\frac{2}{5} + 2\frac{3}{5} =$

2. $5\frac{2}{7} + 6\frac{4}{7} =$

3. $3\frac{3}{8} + 4\frac{1}{8} =$

4. $4\frac{2}{9} + 5\frac{3}{9} =$

5. $6\frac{5}{8} + 7\frac{2}{8} =$

6. $3\frac{3}{8} + 4\frac{1}{8} =$

7. $8\frac{2}{5} + 1\frac{2}{5} =$

8. $7\frac{1}{8} + 7\frac{1}{8} =$

9. $2\frac{3}{4} + 2\frac{1}{4} =$

10. $5\frac{11}{15} + 6\frac{10}{15} =$

11. $2\frac{2}{5} + 2\frac{2}{5} =$

12. $4\frac{3}{4} + 1\frac{1}{4} =$

Adding Mixed Numbers with Like Denominators

Solve each problem. Write the answer in simplest form.

1. $4\frac{5}{8}$
   $+\ 5\frac{4}{8}$

2. $2\frac{2}{5}$
   $+\ 6\frac{4}{5}$

3. $4\frac{5}{8}$
   $+\ 5\frac{4}{8}$

4. $10\frac{3}{4}$
   $+\ 8\frac{2}{4}$

5. $1\frac{1}{2}$
   $+\ 4\frac{1}{2}$

6. $8\frac{4}{9}$
   $+\ 1\frac{5}{9}$

7. $7\frac{6}{9}$
   $+\ 2\frac{1}{9}$

8. $2\frac{5}{6}$
   $+\ 8\frac{5}{6}$

9. $6\frac{2}{3}$
   $+\ 7\frac{2}{3}$

10. $4\frac{2}{7}$
   $+\ 5\frac{3}{7}$

11. $4\frac{2}{5}$
   $+\ 6\frac{4}{5}$

12. $9\frac{4}{12}$
   $+\ 6\frac{10}{12}$

13. $3\frac{9}{10}$
   $+\ 7\frac{6}{10}$

14. $3\frac{1}{3}$
   $+\ 4\frac{2}{3}$

15. $3\frac{1}{3}$
   $+\ 5\frac{2}{3}$

16. $1\frac{4}{5}$
   $+\ 5\frac{3}{5}$

Adding Fractions with Unlike Denominators

Total Problems:	**20**
Problems Correct:	_____

Solve each problem. Write the answer in simplest form.

1. $\dfrac{7}{8}$
$+ \dfrac{1}{4}$

2. $\dfrac{1}{3}$
$+ \dfrac{5}{6}$

3. $\dfrac{5}{12}$
$+ \dfrac{1}{10}$

4. $\dfrac{2}{7}$
$+ \dfrac{1}{5}$

5. $\dfrac{3}{10}$
$+ \dfrac{4}{5}$

6. $\dfrac{1}{12}$
$+ \dfrac{3}{4}$

7. $\dfrac{2}{5}$
$+ \dfrac{5}{10}$

8. $\dfrac{4}{5}$
$+ \dfrac{3}{6}$

9. $\dfrac{1}{4}$
$+ \dfrac{1}{2}$

10. $\dfrac{2}{3}$
$+ \dfrac{4}{9}$

11. $\dfrac{1}{8}$
$+ \dfrac{5}{9}$

12. $\dfrac{2}{7}$
$+ \dfrac{1}{3}$

13. $\dfrac{1}{10}$
$+ \dfrac{4}{8}$

14. $\dfrac{5}{8}$
$+ \dfrac{1}{2}$

15. $\dfrac{2}{3}$
$+ \dfrac{1}{6}$

16. $\dfrac{4}{8}$
$+ \dfrac{3}{7}$

17. $\dfrac{2}{3}$
$+ \dfrac{5}{6}$

18. $\dfrac{5}{12}$
$+ \dfrac{1}{4}$

19. $\dfrac{6}{12}$
$+ \dfrac{7}{13}$

20. $\dfrac{1}{2}$
$+ \dfrac{3}{4}$

Adding Fractions with Unlike Denominators

Solve each problem. Write the answer in simplest form.

1. $\dfrac{2}{5}$
    $+\dfrac{1}{2}$

2. $\dfrac{2}{3}$
    $+\dfrac{3}{4}$

3. $\dfrac{6}{12}$
    $+\dfrac{3}{10}$

4. $\dfrac{2}{6}$
    $+\dfrac{1}{8}$

5. $\dfrac{3}{10}$
    $+\dfrac{1}{3}$

6. $\dfrac{1}{3}$
    $+\dfrac{2}{5}$

7. $\dfrac{2}{6}$
    $+\dfrac{5}{12}$

8. $\dfrac{4}{8}$
    $+\dfrac{3}{5}$

9. $\dfrac{7}{8}$
    $+\dfrac{1}{3}$

10. $\dfrac{5}{6}$
    $+\dfrac{2}{5}$

11. $\dfrac{1}{7}$
    $+\dfrac{5}{8}$

12. $\dfrac{2}{9}$
    $+\dfrac{2}{3}$

13. $\dfrac{2}{10}$
    $+\dfrac{3}{4}$

14. $\dfrac{5}{6}$
    $+\dfrac{1}{4}$

15. $\dfrac{1}{4}$
    $+\dfrac{2}{5}$

16. $\dfrac{2}{4}$
    $+\dfrac{3}{7}$

17. $\dfrac{2}{3}$
    $+\dfrac{4}{5}$

18. $\dfrac{3}{12}$
    $+\dfrac{2}{4}$

19. $\dfrac{5}{13}$
    $+\dfrac{2}{4}$

20. $\dfrac{1}{3}$
    $+\dfrac{3}{6}$

Adding Mixed Numbers with Unlike Denominators

Total Problems: **16**
Problems Correct: _____

Solve each problem. Write the answer in simplest form.

1. $4\frac{5}{8}$
    $+\,3\frac{1}{6}$
    _____

2. $2\frac{5}{6}$
    $+\,6\frac{3}{4}$
    _____

3. $4\frac{5}{8}$
    $+\,5\frac{4}{12}$
    _____

4. $10\frac{3}{8}$
    $+\,3\frac{1}{2}$
    _____

5. $3\frac{2}{5}$
    $+\,2\frac{1}{2}$
    _____

6. $8\frac{5}{7}$
    $+\,9\frac{2}{3}$
    _____

7. $8\frac{2}{3}$
    $+\,1\frac{5}{9}$
    _____

8. $2\frac{3}{4}$
    $+\,7\frac{1}{2}$
    _____

9. $1\frac{7}{9}$
    $+\,4\frac{1}{5}$
    _____

10. $6\frac{5}{6}$
    $+\,2\frac{2}{3}$
    _____

11. $4\frac{2}{14}$
    $+\,6\frac{3}{7}$
    _____

12. $1\frac{1}{4}$
    $+\,5\frac{10}{12}$
    _____

13. $6\frac{3}{10}$
    $+\,7\frac{1}{3}$
    _____

14. $5\frac{4}{5}$
    $+\,3\frac{2}{3}$
    _____

15. $3\frac{1}{6}$
    $+\,4\frac{2}{3}$
    _____

16. $9\frac{1}{2}$
    $+\,8\frac{3}{7}$
    _____

Adding Mixed Numbers with Unlike Denominators

Solve each problem. Write the answer in simplest form.

1. $1\dfrac{3}{8}$
$+\,2\dfrac{1}{2}$
————

2. $3\dfrac{11}{12}$
$+\,4\dfrac{1}{2}$
————

3. $6\dfrac{5}{6}$
$+\,4\dfrac{2}{3}$
————

4. $7\dfrac{2}{3}$
$+\,8\dfrac{4}{5}$
————

5. $5\dfrac{2}{5}$
$+\,3\dfrac{1}{3}$
————

6. $2\dfrac{4}{9}$
$+\,5\dfrac{1}{3}$
————

7. $2\dfrac{2}{7}$
$+\,1\dfrac{1}{3}$
————

8. $2\dfrac{7}{8}$
$+\,4\dfrac{5}{6}$
————

9. $5\dfrac{3}{4}$
$+\,6\dfrac{5}{6}$
————

10. $1\dfrac{3}{4}$
$+\,3\dfrac{2}{3}$
————

11. $4\dfrac{3}{5}$
$+\,5\dfrac{1}{4}$
————

12. $1\dfrac{5}{7}$
$+\,4\dfrac{3}{12}$
————

13. $4\dfrac{7}{12}$
$+\,5\dfrac{1}{2}$
————

14. $10\dfrac{5}{8}$
$+\,2\dfrac{2}{3}$
————

15. $12\dfrac{3}{4}$
$+\,8\dfrac{2}{5}$
————

16. $9\dfrac{1}{8}$
$+\,6\dfrac{3}{4}$
————

Adding Fractions and Mixed Numbers Review

Solve each problem. Write the answer in simplest form.

1. $2\frac{1}{3} + 4\frac{1}{3} =$

2. $2\frac{3}{4} + 7\frac{1}{3} =$

3. $\frac{1}{8} + \frac{1}{4} =$

4. $\frac{3}{7} + \frac{1}{2} =$

5. $\frac{2}{9} + \frac{2}{7} =$

6. $6\frac{1}{9} + 3\frac{2}{9} =$

7. $1\frac{3}{8} + 2\frac{1}{3} =$

8. $\frac{2}{5} + \frac{1}{5} =$

9. $\frac{4}{7} + \frac{1}{7} =$

10. $\frac{5}{7} + \frac{2}{6} =$

11. $1\frac{1}{6} + 2\frac{3}{8} =$

12. $4\frac{10}{12} + 6\frac{11}{15} =$

13. $\frac{3}{3} + \frac{1}{7} =$

14. $\frac{3}{9} + \frac{2}{5} =$

15. $\frac{4}{9} + \frac{9}{9} =$

16. $\frac{1}{2} + \frac{2}{3} =$

17. $\frac{4}{6} + \frac{2}{6} =$

18. $\frac{2}{3} + \frac{1}{5} =$

Adding Fractions and Mixed Numbers Review

Solve each problem. Write the answer in simplest form.

1. $\dfrac{2}{3}$
    $+\dfrac{1}{5}$

2. $\dfrac{4}{5}$
    $+\dfrac{7}{8}$

3. $8\dfrac{1}{3}$
    $+1\dfrac{1}{3}$

4. $11\dfrac{2}{3}$
    $+9\dfrac{1}{5}$

5. $\dfrac{2}{10}$
    $+\dfrac{3}{5}$

6. $\dfrac{1}{10}$
    $+\dfrac{3}{5}$

7. $2\dfrac{4}{8}$
    $+6\dfrac{5}{6}$

8. $3\dfrac{1}{6}$
    $+2\dfrac{3}{6}$

9. $\dfrac{2}{7}$
    $+\dfrac{5}{7}$

10. $\dfrac{4}{5}$
    $+\dfrac{1}{8}$

11. $\dfrac{3}{11}$
    $+\dfrac{4}{8}$

12. $\dfrac{2}{7}$
    $+\dfrac{1}{9}$

13. $4\dfrac{2}{7}$
    $+6\dfrac{3}{7}$

14. $8\dfrac{3}{10}$
    $+3\dfrac{10}{11}$

15. $\dfrac{3}{4}$
    $+\dfrac{1}{4}$

16. $\dfrac{2}{12}$
    $+\dfrac{1}{8}$

17. $2\dfrac{1}{3}$
    $+4\dfrac{2}{5}$

18. $1\dfrac{4}{6}$
    $+5\dfrac{3}{6}$

Subtracting Fractions with Like Denominators

Solve each problem. Write the answer in simplest form.

1. $\dfrac{5}{6}$
$-\dfrac{1}{6}$

2. $\dfrac{7}{12}$
$-\dfrac{5}{12}$

3. $\dfrac{9}{14}$
$-\dfrac{1}{14}$

4. $\dfrac{7}{8}$
$-\dfrac{5}{8}$

5. $\dfrac{6}{8}$
$-\dfrac{3}{8}$

6. $\dfrac{5}{7}$
$-\dfrac{2}{7}$

7. $\dfrac{9}{11}$
$-\dfrac{1}{11}$

8. $\dfrac{5}{9}$
$-\dfrac{4}{9}$

9. $\dfrac{3}{10}$
$-\dfrac{1}{10}$

10. $\dfrac{7}{9}$
$-\dfrac{1}{9}$

11. $\dfrac{5}{8}$
$-\dfrac{1}{8}$

12. $\dfrac{5}{7}$
$-\dfrac{3}{7}$

13. $\dfrac{15}{16}$
$-\dfrac{11}{16}$

14. $\dfrac{4}{5}$
$-\dfrac{2}{5}$

15. $\dfrac{2}{3}$
$-\dfrac{1}{3}$

16. $\dfrac{2}{5}$
$-\dfrac{1}{5}$

17. $\dfrac{3}{4}$
$-\dfrac{1}{4}$

18. $\dfrac{13}{15}$
$-\dfrac{11}{15}$

19. $\dfrac{9}{10}$
$-\dfrac{7}{10}$

20. $\dfrac{3}{3}$
$-\dfrac{1}{3}$

Subtracting Fractions with Like Denominators

Solve each problem. Write the answer in simplest form.

1. $\dfrac{2}{5} - \dfrac{1}{5} =$

2. $\dfrac{5}{9} - \dfrac{2}{9} =$

3. $\dfrac{6}{7} - \dfrac{1}{7} =$

4. $\dfrac{5}{6} - \dfrac{3}{6} =$

5. $\dfrac{2}{9} - \dfrac{2}{9} =$

6. $\dfrac{7}{9} - \dfrac{3}{9} =$

7. $\dfrac{5}{10} - \dfrac{2}{10} =$

8. $\dfrac{5}{5} - \dfrac{2}{5} =$

9. $\dfrac{9}{20} - \dfrac{2}{20} =$

10. $\dfrac{2}{2} - \dfrac{1}{2} =$

11. $\dfrac{3}{8} - \dfrac{2}{8} =$

12. $\dfrac{2}{3} - \dfrac{1}{3} =$

13. $\dfrac{3}{4} - \dfrac{2}{4} =$

14. $\dfrac{1}{7} - \dfrac{1}{7} =$

15. $\dfrac{1}{1} - \dfrac{1}{1} =$

Subtracting Fractions from Whole Numbers

| Total Problems: | **20** |
| Problems Correct: | _____ |

Solve each problem. Write the answer in simplest form.

1. 2
$-\dfrac{7}{8}$

2. 4
$-\dfrac{3}{10}$

3. 12
$-\dfrac{5}{7}$

4. 5
$-\dfrac{1}{4}$

5. 4
$-\dfrac{3}{5}$

6. 5
$-\dfrac{6}{9}$

7. 9
$-\dfrac{1}{3}$

8. 4
$-\dfrac{2}{6}$

9. 3
$-\dfrac{3}{4}$

10. 4
$-\dfrac{3}{6}$

11. 4
$-\dfrac{7}{8}$

12. 3
$-\dfrac{2}{3}$

13. 8
$-\dfrac{9}{9}$

14. 5
$-\dfrac{2}{5}$

15. 3
$-\dfrac{6}{7}$

16. 2
$-\dfrac{6}{8}$

17. 7
$-\dfrac{4}{5}$

18. 10
$-\dfrac{1}{2}$

19. 6
$-\dfrac{1}{6}$

20. 1
$-\dfrac{3}{5}$

Name _____   Date _____

Subtracting Fractions from Whole Numbers

Solve each problem. Write the answer in simplest form.

1. $15 - \dfrac{3}{8}$

2. $9 - \dfrac{3}{11}$

3. $12 - \dfrac{3}{5}$

4. $4 - \dfrac{1}{2}$

5. $10 - \dfrac{2}{5}$

6. $14 - \dfrac{2}{9}$

7. $6 - \dfrac{1}{5}$

8. $2 - \dfrac{1}{6}$

9. $1 - \dfrac{1}{3}$

10. $13 - \dfrac{2}{3}$

11. $7 - \dfrac{5}{6}$

12. $2 - \dfrac{4}{5}$

13. $2 - \dfrac{6}{11}$

14. $1 - \dfrac{7}{8}$

15. $5 - \dfrac{1}{4}$

16. $6 - \dfrac{6}{9}$

17. $5 - \dfrac{3}{5}$

18. $10 - \dfrac{1}{3}$

19. $8 - \dfrac{3}{4}$

20. $7 - \dfrac{3}{7}$

Subtracting Mixed Numbers with Like Denominators

Total Problems: **16**
Problems Correct: _____

Solve each problem. Write the answer in simplest form.

1. $5\frac{5}{8}$
   $-2\frac{4}{8}$

2. $4\frac{2}{6}$
   $-3\frac{5}{6}$

3. $5\frac{5}{8}$
   $-3\frac{4}{8}$

4. $7\frac{3}{5}$
   $-5\frac{1}{5}$

5. $8\frac{4}{5}$
   $-4\frac{1}{5}$

6. $3\frac{2}{6}$
   $-2\frac{1}{6}$

7. $9\frac{6}{7}$
   $-2\frac{2}{7}$

8. $8\frac{7}{9}$
   $-8\frac{6}{9}$

9. $5\frac{2}{3}$
   $-1\frac{1}{3}$

10. $10\frac{3}{4}$
    $-7\frac{1}{4}$

11. $5\frac{3}{3}$
    $-4\frac{2}{3}$

12. $4\frac{9}{10}$
    $-2\frac{7}{10}$

13. $3\frac{2}{10}$
    $-1\frac{2}{10}$

14. $6\frac{7}{8}$
    $-1\frac{1}{8}$

15. $2\frac{1}{8}$
    $-1\frac{1}{8}$

16. $2\frac{3}{5}$
    $-1\frac{4}{5}$

Subtracting Mixed Numbers with Like Denominators

Total Problems: **16**
Problems Correct: _____

Solve each problem. Write the answer in simplest form.

1. $12\frac{7}{8}$
$-\ 5\frac{5}{8}$

2. $2\frac{2}{3}$
$-\ 2\frac{1}{3}$

3. $9\frac{7}{8}$
$-\ 4\frac{4}{8}$

4. $3\frac{1}{8}$
$-\ 1\frac{7}{8}$

5. $10\frac{2}{5}$
$-\ 7\frac{4}{5}$

6. $3\frac{1}{4}$
$-\ 2\frac{3}{4}$

7. $10\frac{2}{3}$
$-\ 9\frac{1}{3}$

8. $5\frac{4}{5}$
$-\ 4\frac{1}{5}$

9. $5\frac{2}{3}$
$-\ 1\frac{1}{3}$

10. $8\frac{7}{10}$
$-\ 7\frac{9}{10}$

11. $8\frac{3}{16}$
$-\ 7\frac{5}{16}$

12. $6\frac{7}{15}$
$-\ 2\frac{8}{15}$

13. $6\frac{2}{12}$
$-\ 3\frac{2}{12}$

14. $4\frac{5}{6}$
$-\ 2\frac{1}{6}$

15. $4\frac{11}{18}$
$-\ 1\frac{7}{18}$

16. $8\frac{7}{10}$
$-\ 1\frac{3}{10}$

Subtracting Fractions with Unlike Denominators

Solve each problem. Write the answer in simplest form.

1. $\dfrac{1}{3}$
   $-\dfrac{1}{4}$

2. $\dfrac{3}{4}$
   $-\dfrac{1}{5}$

3. $\dfrac{9}{10}$
   $-\dfrac{5}{7}$

4. $\dfrac{5}{7}$
   $-\dfrac{2}{9}$

5. $\dfrac{3}{5}$
   $-\dfrac{1}{3}$

6. $\dfrac{3}{8}$
   $-\dfrac{2}{6}$

7. $\dfrac{2}{4}$
   $-\dfrac{1}{3}$

8. $\dfrac{1}{5}$
   $-\dfrac{1}{8}$

9. $\dfrac{7}{12}$
   $-\dfrac{1}{4}$

10. $\dfrac{3}{9}$
    $-\dfrac{1}{4}$

11. $\dfrac{7}{8}$
    $-\dfrac{1}{9}$

12. $\dfrac{8}{8}$
    $-\dfrac{4}{6}$

13. $\dfrac{2}{3}$
    $-\dfrac{1}{2}$

14. $\dfrac{2}{3}$
    $-\dfrac{4}{9}$

15. $\dfrac{1}{3}$
    $-\dfrac{1}{6}$

16. $\dfrac{8}{9}$
    $-\dfrac{3}{6}$

17. $\dfrac{5}{6}$
    $-\dfrac{1}{5}$

18. $\dfrac{7}{8}$
    $-\dfrac{3}{10}$

19. $\dfrac{9}{12}$
    $-\dfrac{2}{11}$

20. $\dfrac{6}{6}$
    $-\dfrac{3}{12}$

Subtracting Fractions with Unlike Denominators

Solve each problem. Write the answer in simplest form.

1. $\dfrac{3}{4}$
    $-\dfrac{1}{6}$

2. $\dfrac{13}{15}$
    $-\dfrac{2}{3}$

3. $\dfrac{2}{3}$
    $-\dfrac{7}{12}$

4. $\dfrac{5}{6}$
    $-\dfrac{1}{3}$

5. $\dfrac{5}{6}$
    $-\dfrac{2}{5}$

6. $\dfrac{2}{3}$
    $-\dfrac{1}{6}$

7. $\dfrac{11}{14}$
    $-\dfrac{1}{2}$

8. $\dfrac{7}{12}$
    $-\dfrac{1}{4}$

9. $\dfrac{11}{12}$
    $-\dfrac{1}{6}$

10. $\dfrac{5}{6}$
    $-\dfrac{3}{7}$

11. $\dfrac{7}{8}$
    $-\dfrac{1}{9}$

12. $\dfrac{5}{6}$
    $-\dfrac{1}{2}$

13. $\dfrac{5}{12}$
    $-\dfrac{1}{3}$

14. $\dfrac{7}{8}$
    $-\dfrac{1}{6}$

15. $\dfrac{1}{3}$
    $-\dfrac{1}{6}$

16. $\dfrac{2}{3}$
    $-\dfrac{4}{9}$

17. $\dfrac{3}{4}$
    $-\dfrac{1}{3}$

18. $\dfrac{8}{9}$
    $-\dfrac{5}{6}$

19. $\dfrac{9}{12}$
    $-\dfrac{2}{11}$

20. $\dfrac{5}{6}$
    $-\dfrac{1}{8}$

Subtracting Mixed Numbers with Unlike Denominators

Total Problems: **16**
Problems Correct: _____

Solve each problem. Write the answer in simplest form.

1. $2\frac{2}{3}$
   $-1\frac{1}{2}$

2. $4\frac{1}{3}$
   $-2\frac{3}{8}$

3. $3\frac{5}{6}$
   $-2\frac{1}{12}$

4. $5\frac{5}{8}$
   $-2\frac{3}{4}$

5. $4\frac{7}{10}$
   $-1\frac{2}{5}$

6. $3\frac{7}{8}$
   $-2\frac{1}{6}$

7. $5\frac{4}{9}$
   $-2\frac{1}{3}$

8. $3\frac{1}{2}$
   $-1\frac{3}{4}$

9. $4\frac{1}{3}$
   $-1\frac{2}{5}$

10. $5\frac{5}{12}$
    $-3\frac{7}{10}$

11. $3\frac{5}{6}$
    $-1\frac{5}{9}$

12. $7\frac{3}{5}$
    $-4\frac{7}{10}$

13. $6\frac{2}{4}$
    $-4\frac{1}{2}$

14. $4\frac{7}{8}$
    $-2\frac{1}{4}$

15. $4\frac{2}{5}$
    $-2\frac{3}{10}$

16. $6\frac{4}{5}$
    $-5\frac{3}{7}$

Subtracting Mixed Numbers with Unlike Denominators

Solve each problem. Write the answer in simplest form.

1. $5\frac{1}{6}$
    $-2\frac{3}{4}$

2. $4\frac{7}{10}$
    $-1\frac{4}{5}$

3. $5\frac{7}{8}$
    $-1\frac{1}{16}$

4. $3\frac{1}{3}$
    $-1\frac{5}{6}$

5. $4\frac{1}{3}$
    $-1\frac{1}{4}$

6. $3\frac{7}{12}$
    $-1\frac{9}{10}$

7. $5\frac{4}{5}$
    $-1\frac{9}{10}$

8. $4\frac{3}{4}$
    $-1\frac{5}{6}$

9. $6\frac{1}{2}$
    $-\frac{1}{3}$

10. $7\frac{1}{4}$
    $-3\frac{2}{3}$

11. $10\frac{4}{5}$
    $-6\frac{5}{6}$

12. $12\frac{2}{3}$
    $-9\frac{6}{7}$

13. $5\frac{1}{3}$
    $-3\frac{3}{4}$

14. $8\frac{2}{5}$
    $-4\frac{1}{4}$

15. $2\frac{2}{3}$
    $-2\frac{1}{4}$

16. $6\frac{1}{3}$
    $-5\frac{3}{4}$

Multiplying Fractions

Solve each problem. Write the answer in simplest form.

1. $\dfrac{3}{4} \times \dfrac{2}{5} =$ **2.** $\dfrac{7}{8} \times \dfrac{1}{6} =$ **3.** $\dfrac{4}{5} \times \dfrac{2}{3} =$

4. $\dfrac{1}{3} \times \dfrac{1}{5} =$ **5.** $\dfrac{2}{7} \times \dfrac{2}{9} =$ **6.** $\dfrac{1}{4} \times \dfrac{3}{5} =$

7. $\dfrac{4}{7} \times \dfrac{3}{8} =$ **8.** $\dfrac{2}{3} \times \dfrac{2}{5} =$ **9.** $\dfrac{2}{3} \times \dfrac{4}{5} =$

10. $\dfrac{3}{5} \times \dfrac{1}{3} =$ **11.** $\dfrac{1}{8} \times \dfrac{2}{5} =$ **12.** $\dfrac{1}{6} \times \dfrac{2}{3} =$

13. $\dfrac{1}{2} \times \dfrac{3}{4} =$ **14.** $\dfrac{1}{8} \times \dfrac{1}{3} =$ **15.** $\dfrac{1}{6} \times \dfrac{4}{5} =$

Multiplying Fractions

Solve each problem. Write the answer in simplest form.

1. $\dfrac{1}{3} \times \dfrac{1}{7} =$

2. $\dfrac{3}{5} \times \dfrac{2}{9} =$

3. $\dfrac{1}{6} \times \dfrac{4}{5} =$

4. $\dfrac{2}{7} \times \dfrac{5}{8} =$

5. $\dfrac{2}{5} \times \dfrac{4}{9} =$

6. $\dfrac{1}{4} \times \dfrac{1}{6} =$

7. $\dfrac{2}{3} \times \dfrac{3}{8} =$

8. $\dfrac{3}{4} \times \dfrac{4}{7} =$

9. $\dfrac{2}{5} \times \dfrac{5}{6} =$

10. $\dfrac{4}{5} \times \dfrac{2}{3} =$

11. $\dfrac{1}{5} \times \dfrac{5}{6} =$

12. $\dfrac{1}{2} \times \dfrac{3}{7} =$

13. $\dfrac{2}{5} \times \dfrac{4}{9} =$

14. $\dfrac{2}{8} \times \dfrac{3}{3} =$

15. $\dfrac{1}{7} \times \dfrac{6}{8} =$

Multiplying Fractions and Whole Numbers

Solve each problem. Write the answer in simplest form.

1. $4 \times \frac{1}{2} =$

2. $2 \times \frac{2}{5} =$

3. $4 \times \frac{2}{7} =$

4. $3 \times \frac{5}{6} =$

5. $8 \times \frac{1}{8} =$

6. $\frac{2}{5} \times 3 =$

7. $\frac{1}{8} \times 5 =$

8. $\frac{5}{7} \times 5 =$

9. $\frac{2}{3} \times 2 =$

10. $\frac{3}{9} \times 4 =$

11. $\frac{1}{3} \times 7 =$

12. $4 \times \frac{3}{4} =$

13. $\frac{6}{8} \times 2 =$

14. $5 \times \frac{4}{5} =$

15. $3 \times \frac{2}{3} =$

Multiplying Fractions and Whole Numbers

Solve each problem. Write the answer in simplest form.

1. $5 \times \dfrac{2}{5} =$

2. $8 \times \dfrac{1}{7} =$

3. $6 \times \dfrac{3}{8} =$

4. $4 \times \dfrac{8}{9} =$

5. $2 \times \dfrac{3}{7} =$

6. $\dfrac{2}{3} \times 4 =$

7. $\dfrac{1}{9} \times 6 =$

8. $\dfrac{5}{6} \times 4 =$

9. $\dfrac{4}{6} \times 3 =$

10. $\dfrac{4}{5} \times 6 =$

11. $\dfrac{3}{4} \times 5 =$

12. $2 \times \dfrac{4}{5} =$

13. $\dfrac{2}{7} \times 6 =$

14. $7 \times \dfrac{3}{5} =$

15. $7 \times \dfrac{5}{6} =$

Multiplying Fractions and Whole Numbers

Total Problems: **15**
Problems Correct: _____

Solve each problem. Write the answer in simplest form.

1. $10 \times \dfrac{2}{3} =$

2. $4 \times \dfrac{4}{7} =$

3. $7 \times \dfrac{10}{11} =$

4. $36 \times \dfrac{2}{288} =$

5. $6 \times \dfrac{4}{8} =$

6. $9 \times \dfrac{5}{6} =$

7. $3 \times \dfrac{1}{3} =$

8. $30 \times \dfrac{3}{90} =$

9. $12 \times \dfrac{1}{36} =$

10. $5 \times \dfrac{2}{5} =$

11. $12 \times \dfrac{7}{8} =$

12. $5 \times \dfrac{3}{4} =$

13. $22 \times \dfrac{1}{44} =$

14. $4 \times \dfrac{1}{8} =$

15. $8 \times \dfrac{2}{3} =$

Multiplying Mixed Numbers and Whole Numbers

Solve each problem. Write the answer in simplest form.

1. $2 \times 2\frac{1}{3} =$

2. $3 \times 5\frac{1}{5} =$

3. $9 \times 3\frac{2}{3} =$

4. $8 \times 9\frac{1}{10} =$

5. $4 \times 5\frac{1}{8} =$

6. $6 \times 3\frac{1}{6} =$

7. $5 \times 6\frac{5}{8} =$

8. $3 \times 9\frac{1}{3} =$

9. $7 \times 1\frac{3}{4} =$

10. $7 \times 2\frac{3}{5} =$

11. $4 \times 2\frac{1}{2} =$

12. $7 \times 2\frac{1}{7} =$

Name _____ Date _____

Multiplying Mixed Numbers and Whole Numbers

Solve each problem. Write the answer in simplest form.

1. $4 \times 3\frac{3}{5} =$

2. $6 \times 9\frac{4}{5} =$

3. $2 \times 8\frac{3}{4} =$

4. $9 \times 1\frac{1}{18} =$

5. $10 \times 5\frac{1}{2} =$

6. $8 \times 2\frac{3}{8} =$

7. $5 \times 4\frac{2}{5} =$

8. $2 \times 7\frac{5}{8} =$

9. $2 \times 5\frac{1}{8} =$

10. $3 \times 1\frac{15}{16} =$

11. $4 \times 8\frac{6}{7} =$

12. $2 \times 2\frac{1}{4} =$

Multiplying Mixed Numbers

Solve each problem. Write the answer in simplest form.

1. $3\frac{1}{2} \times 2\frac{1}{2} =$

2. $8\frac{5}{6} \times 3\frac{6}{7} =$

3. $4\frac{2}{5} \times 6\frac{2}{3} =$

4. $4\frac{2}{9} \times 5\frac{10}{11} =$

5. $2\frac{2}{3} \times 4\frac{2}{5} =$

6. $5\frac{3}{4} \times 6\frac{1}{4} =$

7. $2\frac{8}{9} \times 7\frac{7}{8} =$

8. $7\frac{1}{4} \times 3\frac{3}{7} =$

9. $6\frac{7}{8} \times 3\frac{1}{3} =$

10. $7\frac{9}{10} \times 8\frac{7}{8} =$

11. $4\frac{1}{4} \times 3\frac{5}{6} =$

12. $8\frac{3}{5} \times 1\frac{1}{2} =$

Multiplying Mixed Numbers

Solve each problem. Write the answer in simplest form.

1. $8\frac{1}{4} \times 6\frac{2}{3} =$

2. $7\frac{2}{5} \times 6\frac{2}{3} =$

3. $2\frac{5}{6} \times 12\frac{4}{5} =$

4. $4\frac{2}{7} \times 6\frac{1}{10} =$

5. $5\frac{1}{5} \times 4\frac{1}{3} =$

6. $9\frac{9}{10} \times 4\frac{7}{8} =$

7. $1\frac{10}{13} \times 2\frac{9}{13} =$

8. $8\frac{3}{5} \times 4\frac{5}{6} =$

Adding Decimals

Solve each problem. Regroup when necessary.

1. 14.2
    + 12.1

2. 18.7
    + 10.5

3.   1.47
    + 6.54

4. 12.3
    + 15.2

5. 16.6
    + 13.8

6. 7.85
    + 9.41

7. 18.2
    + 16.5

8. 15.2
    + 13.0

9. 2.22
    + 3.94

10. 22.2
    + 13.1

11. 12.0
    + 14.9

12. 7.54
    + 2.24

13. 47.5
    + 32.6

14. 49.4
    + 11.1

15. 8.85
    + 7.33

16. 54.8
    + 13.2

17. 4.58
    + 2.31

18. $12.95 + 5.06 =$

19. $13.8 + 6.9 =$

20. $46.02 + 75.67 =$

21. $16.3 + 35.7 =$

22. $3.25 + 3.25 =$

23. $87.01 + 16.53 =$

Adding Decimals

Solve each problem. Regroup when necessary.

1.   4.15
   6.20
+ 8.63

2.   8.461
  0.003
+ 0.212

3.   33.421
  7.35
+ 42.6

4.   2.26
  3.43
+ 8.15

5.   0.491
 0.320
+ 0.617

6. 22.444
 1.908
+ 0.076

7. 32.15
64.23
+ 32.57

8. 14.501
62.037
+ 8.693

9. 62.561
 0.179
+ 2.602

10. 3.564
 1.508
+ 1.521

11. 62.715
 1.307
+ 0.032

12. 16.201
 7.35
+ 2.9

13. 8.16 + 15.204 + 35.8 =

14. 0.007 + 1.12 + 5.978 =

Subtracting Decimals

Total Problems: **17**
Problems Correct: _____

Solve each problem. Regroup when necessary.

1.   5.6
       − 3.2

2.   10.4
       − 8.2

3.   8.5
       − 3.5

4.   7.8
       − 4.5

5.   9.3
       − 7.5

6.   86.5
       − 2.3

7.   6.3
       − 4.1

8.   8.7
       − 5.2

9.   9.65
       − 4.22

10.   8.6
        − 5.2

11.   16.4
        − 8.2

12.   75.4
        − 3.1

13.   7.6
        − 3.2

14.   26.7
        − 2.5

15.   16.2
        − 4.1

16. 72.5 − 63.7 =

17. 8.1 − 6.5 =

CD-104321 • © Carson-Dellosa

Subtracting Decimals

Solve each problem. Regroup when necessary.

1. 326.7
      – 42.8

2. 14.021
      – 5.6

3. 1.589
      – 0.756

4. 16.882
      – 9.3

5. 52.07
      – 3.9

6. 7.57
      – 6.85

7. 8.123
      – 6.017

8. 18.9
      – 16.425

9. 1.978
      – 1.682

10. 14.9
       – 3.2

11. 19.5 – 0.001 =

12. 0.501 – 0.332 =

13. 42.642 – 10.35 =

14. 28.4 – 4.62 =

15. 33.45 – 15.4 =

16. 18.5 – 9.5 =

Multiplying Decimals

Solve each problem. Regroup when necessary.

1. 5.2
   × 1.8

2. 10.5
   × 6.6

3. 2.8
   × 9.9

4. 2.2
   × 4.4

5. 0.12
   × 3.7

6. 5.20
   × 0.21

7. 1.3
   × 1.0

8. 7.1
   × 0.25

9. 7.54
   × 2.77

10. 6.4
    × 2.5

11. 16.2
    × 1.1

12. 2.0
    × 2.1

13. 5.4
    × 1.3

14. 6.6
    × 1.5

15. 4.44
    × 0.01

16. 0.34
    × 0.12

17. 45.5
    × 4.6

18. 6.1
    × 2.5

19. 5.6
    × 7.3

20. 33.1
    × 0.8

Dividing Decimals

Solve each problem.

1. $2\overline{)8.44}$

2. $5\overline{)1.25}$

3. $14\overline{)1.218}$

4. $2\overline{)38.6}$

5. $67\overline{)0.6566}$

6. $52\overline{)166.4}$

7. $7\overline{)3.92}$

8. $2\overline{)9.4}$

9. $24\overline{)17.28}$

10. $6\overline{)3.6}$

11. $7\overline{)3.92}$

12. $46\overline{)0.2346}$

13. $3\overline{)42.3}$

14. $5\overline{)0.7255}$

15. $10\overline{)166}$

16. $4\overline{)9.6}$

17. $5\overline{)0.865}$

18. $67\overline{)274.7}$

Dividing Decimals

Solve each problem.

1. $0.8 \overline{)64}$

2. $0.25 \overline{)100}$

3. $6.1 \overline{)7.93}$

4. $0.5 \overline{)35}$

5. $1.2 \overline{)48}$

6. $5.3 \overline{)42.4}$

7. $0.4 \overline{)64}$

8. $0.7 \overline{)4.9}$

9. $0.19 \overline{)15.2}$

10. $0.3 \overline{)9}$

11. $9.6 \overline{)82.8}$

12. $0.17 \overline{)3.23}$

13. $0.8 \overline{)152}$

14. $0.3 \overline{)0.63}$

15. $2.1 \overline{)1.365}$

16. $0.12 \overline{)360}$

17. $0.23 \overline{)2.185}$

18. $7.2 \overline{)40.32}$

Writing Decimals as Fractions

Write each decimal as a fraction in simplest form.

1. $0.5 =$

2. $0.9 =$

3. $0.7 =$

4. $9.5 =$

5. $1.8 =$

6. $2.2 =$

7. $6.2 =$

8. $1.25 =$

9. $0.1 =$

10. $0.22 =$

11. $4.1 =$

12. $3.6 =$

13. $7.3 =$

14. $3.9 =$

15. $8.8 =$

16. $2.5 =$

17. $0.4 =$

18. $0.8 =$

19. $5.2 =$

20. $2.5 =$

21. $6.5 =$

22. $4.2 =$

23. $4.1 =$

24. $9.3 =$

Writing Decimals as Fractions

Write each decimal as a fraction in simplest form.

1. 8.2 =

2. 5.4 =

3. 48.2 =

4. 0.15 =

5. 25.32 =

6. 3.25 =

7. 30.2 =

8. 0.625 =

9. 9.1 =

10. 10.6 =

11. 0.25 =

12. 0.68 =

13. 86.12 =

14. 6.5 =

15. 9.12 =

16. 0.125 =

17. 7.6 =

18. 25.3 =

19. 0.75 =

20. 4.36 =

21. 9.45 =

22. 75.2 =

23. 25.2 =

24. 25.6 =

Writing Fractions as Decimals

Write each fraction as a decimal. Round to the nearest thousandth when necessary.

1. $\dfrac{5}{8} =$

2. $\dfrac{1}{8} =$

3. $\dfrac{1}{5} =$

4. $\dfrac{1}{12} =$

5. $\dfrac{1}{20} =$

6. $\dfrac{5}{9} =$

7. $\dfrac{1}{4} =$

8. $\dfrac{7}{8} =$

9. $\dfrac{4}{5} =$

10. $\dfrac{2}{7} =$

11. $\dfrac{3}{5} =$

12. $\dfrac{3}{6} =$

13. $\dfrac{3}{4} =$

14. $\dfrac{5}{6} =$

15. $\dfrac{9}{10} =$

16. $\dfrac{11}{20} =$

17. $\dfrac{1}{6} =$

18. $\dfrac{7}{8} =$

Name _____ Date _____

Writing Fractions as Decimals
and Decimals as Fractions

Complete the chart. Round to the nearest thousandth when necessary.

	Fraction	Decimal
1.		0.125
2.	$\dfrac{1}{4}$	
3.		0.834
4.	$\dfrac{1}{7}$	
5.		0.9
6.	$\dfrac{3}{8}$	
7.		0.56
8.	$\dfrac{7}{8}$	
9.		0.2
10.	$\dfrac{10}{11}$	

Learning About Lines and Line Segments

Circle the correct name for each figure.

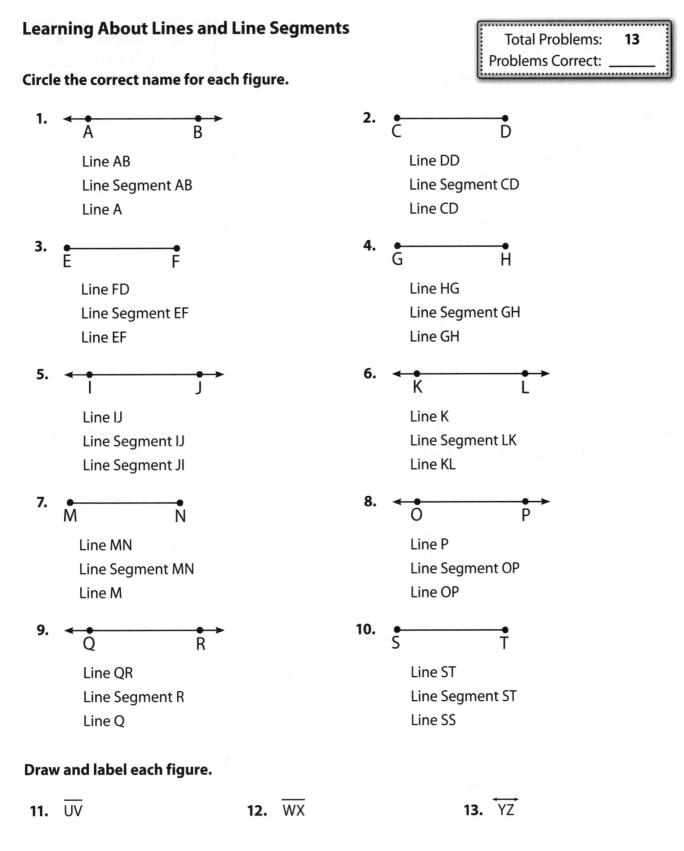

1.

   A   B

Line AB
Line Segment AB
Line A

2.

   C   D

Line DD
Line Segment CD
Line CD

3.

   E   F

Line FD
Line Segment EF
Line EF

4.

   G   H

Line HG
Line Segment GH
Line GH

5.

   I   J

Line IJ
Line Segment IJ
Line Segment JI

6.

   K   L

Line K
Line Segment LK
Line KL

7.

   M   N

Line MN
Line Segment MN
Line M

8.

   O   P

Line P
Line Segment OP
Line OP

9.

   Q   R

Line QR
Line Segment R
Line Q

10.

   S   T

Line ST
Line Segment ST
Line SS

Draw and label each figure.

11. $\overline{UV}$

12. $\overline{WX}$

13. $\overleftrightarrow{YZ}$

Naming Angles

Circle the correct name for each angle.

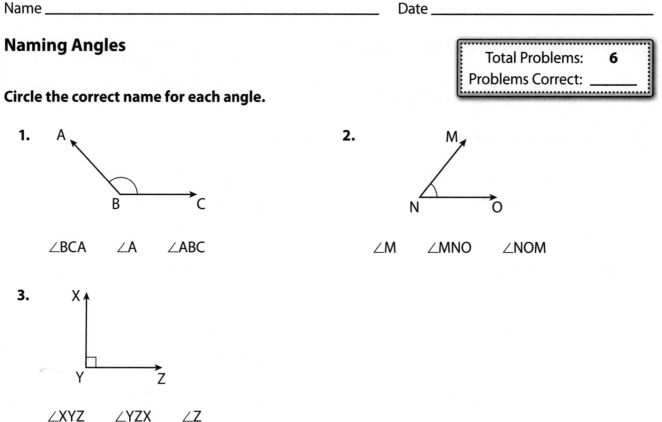

1.   A

B   C

∠BCA   ∠A   ∠ABC

2.   M

N   O

∠M   ∠MNO   ∠NOM

3.   X

Y   Z

∠XYZ   ∠YZX   ∠Z

Name each angle below in the first space. Use a protractor to measure each angle and write the measurement in the second space.

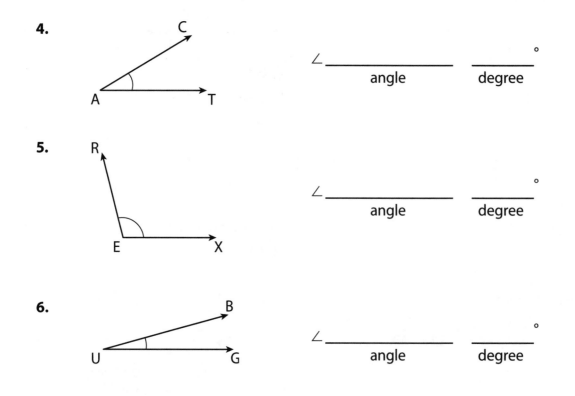

4.   C

A   T

∠ _____   _____ °
         angle   degree

5.   R

E   X

∠ _____   _____ °
         angle   degree

6.   B

U   G

∠ _____   _____ °
         angle   degree

Naming Polygons

Write the number of sides of each figure.

1.

_____

2.

_____

3.

_____

4.

_____

5.

_____

6.

_____

Draw each polygon.

7.   pentagon

8.   octagon

9.   hexagon

10.   quadrilateral

Name _____   Date _____

Naming Circles and Polygons

Circle the correct name for the labeled part of each figure.

1.

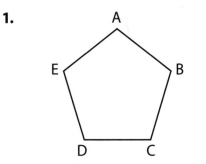

   a. Hexagon ABCDE

   b. Pentagon ABCDE

   c. Pentagon DABEC

2.

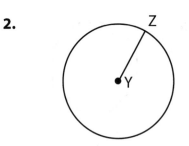

   a. Circle Z

   b. Line Segment YZ

   c. Radius YZ

3.

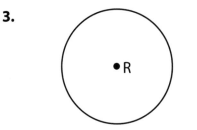

   a. Circle R

   b. Radius R

   c. Line R

4. **Draw a hexagon and label it UVWXYZ.**

5. **Label the circle according to the instructions.**

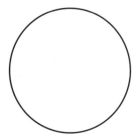

   a) Draw a point in the middle of the circle. Label it M.
   b) Draw a radius. Label it MO.
   c) Draw a diameter. Label it PQ.
   d) Label the circle. Write the label above the circle.

Standard and Metric Length

Total Problems:	**24**
Problems Correct:	_____

Write the correct abbreviation for each measurement in the blank.

1. _____ centimeter

2. _____ yard

3. _____ foot

4. _____ kilometer

5. _____ inch

6. _____ meter

7. _____ mile

8. _____ millimeter

m
cm
mm
in.
yd.
mi.
ft.
km

Give the equivalent for each measurement.

9. 1 yd. = _____ in.

10. 1 m = _____ cm

11. 1 mi. = _____ ft.

12. 1 cm = _____ m

13. 1 yd. = _____ ft.

14. 1 km = _____ m

15. 1 mi. = _____ yd.

16. 1,000 m = _____ km

17. 6 ft. = _____ in.

18. 5 km = _____ m

19. 3 mi. = _____ yd.

20. 9 cm = _____ mm

21. 2 yd. = _____ in.

22. 300 mm = _____ cm

23. 72 in. = _____ ft.

24. 1 m = _____ km

Name _____ Date _____

Standard Length

Give the equivalent for each measurement.

1. 4 ft. = _____ in.

2. 84 in. = _____ ft.

3. 33 yd. = _____ ft.

4. 36 in. = _____ ft.

5. 12 yd. = _____ ft.

6. 9 ft. = _____ in.

7. 48 ft. = _____ yd.

8. 24 ft. = _____ yd.

9. 3 mi. = _____ yd.

10. 108 in. = _____ yd.

11. 7 yd. = _____ ft.

12. 21 ft. = _____ yd.

Solve each problem.

13. Leslie ran 3,520 yards. How many miles did she run?

14. Anita has 7 yards of fabric. How many feet of fabric does she have?

15. Brian needs 108 inches of pipe. How many feet of pipe does he need to buy?

16. Tess has 180 inches of ribbon. She uses 36 inches. How many yards of ribbon does she have left?

Name _____ Date _____

Metric Length

Give the equivalent for each measurement.

1. 5 cm = _____ mm

2. 700 cm = _____ m

3. 8,000 m = _____ km

4. 16,000 m = _____ km

5. 60 mm = _____ cm

6. 36 cm = _____ mm

7. 400 cm = _____ m

8. 2 km = _____ m

9. 15 m = _____ cm

10. 90 mm = _____ cm

11. 72 m = _____ cm

12. 4 km = _____ m

13. 9 m = _____ cm

14. 5,000 m = _____ km

15. 84 cm = _____ mm

16. 17 km = _____ m

17. 3 cm = _____ mm

18. 61 m = _____ cm

19. 55 cm = _____ mm

20. 2 km = _____ cm

21. 30,000 cm = _____ km

Solve each problem.

22. Penny walked 2 kilometers. Anita walked 5,000 meters. How many more meters did Anita walk than Penny?

23. Norman has a piece of string that measures 15 centimeters. Kayla has a piece of string that measures 200 millimeters. Who has the longer piece of string?

Standard Capacity

Total Problems: **17**
Problems Correct: _____

Give the equivalent for each measurement.

1. 2 tbsp. = _____ tsp.

2. 12 c. = _____ pt.

3. 3 gal. = _____ pt.

4. 2 pt. = _____ c.

5. 5 tbsp. = _____ tsp.

6. 8 qt. = _____ pt.

7. 9 tbsp. = _____ tsp.

8. 14 pt. = _____ qt.

9. 7 pt. = _____ c.

10. 10 qt. = _____ pt.

11. 8 qt. = _____ gal.

12. 12 pt. = _____ qt.

13. 14 pt. = _____ c.

14. 3 tbsp. = _____ tsp.

15. 24 c. = _____ pt.

Solve each problem.

16. If Lindsay has 2 gallons of milk, how many pints does she have?

17. Jeff is making orange juice. If he has 8 quarts, how many 1-cup servings can he pour?

Metric Capacity

Give the equivalent for each measurement.

1. 8 L = _____ mL

2. 5,000 mL = _____ L

3. 15 L = _____ mL

4. 48,000 mL = _____ L

5. 0.4 L = _____ mL

6. 33,000 mL = _____ L

7. 92 L = _____ mL

8. 2.1 L = _____ mL

9. 7,000 mL = _____ L

10. 6 L = _____ mL

11. 800 mL = _____ L

12. 27 L = _____ mL

Solve each problem.

13. William measures 18,000 milliliters of milk. How many liters does he measure?

14. Karen drinks 0.5 liter of soft drink. How many milliliters does she drink?

15. Mark pours 14 liters of juice at the party. How many milliliters of juice does he pour?

16. Isabelle buys fifteen 2-liter bottles of soft drink for the party. Her guests drink 18,000 milliliters. How many liters of soft drink does Isabelle have left?

Standard Mass

Give the equivalent for each measurement.

1. 4 lb. = _____ oz.

2. 1 lb. 25 oz. = _____ oz.

3. 64 oz. = _____ lb.

4. 1,200 oz. = _____ lb.

5. 96,000 oz. = _____ tn.

6. 6,000 lb. = _____ tn.

7. 22 lb. = _____ oz.

8. 4.5 lb. = _____ oz.

9. 32 oz. = _____ lb.

10. 96 oz. = _____ lb.

11. 144 oz. = _____ lb.

12. 160 oz. = _____ lb.

13. 2 tn. = _____ oz.

14. 3 lb. 4 oz. = _____ oz.

15. 3.5 tn. = _____ lb.

Solve each problem.

16. A produce truck that carries apples and oranges weighs 4 tons. How much does the truck weigh in pounds?

17. Vera's game weighs $\frac{1}{2}$ pound. How many ounces does her game weigh?

18. Jan's recipe calls for 1 pound of sugar. How many total ounces does she need?

19. Meredith lifts two 5-pound weights every day. How many total ounces does she lift?

Metric Mass

Give the equivalent for each measurement.

1. 3 g = _____ mg

2. 8,000 mg = _____ g

3. 14,000 g = _____ kg

4. 84,000 g = _____ kg

5. 9 g = _____ mg

6. 650,000 mg = _____ kg

7. 73 g = _____ mg

8. 0.8 kg = _____ mg

9. 25,000 g = _____ kg

10. 7,000 g = _____ kg

11. 12 g = _____ mg

12. 118,000 g = _____ kg

13. 6,000 g = _____ kg

14. 2,000 mg = _____ g

15. 65 g = _____ mg

Solve each problem.

16. Megan uses 4,000 milligrams of sugar in her recipe. How many grams of sugar does she use?

17. Harry measures 15 grams of salt. How many milligrams does he measure?

18. Jake's book weighs 2 kilograms. How many grams does his book weigh?

19. Peter's recipe calls for 16,000 milligrams of cocoa. How many grams of cocoa does Peter need?

Finding the Perimeter

Find the perimeter of each figure. Remember to write the units.

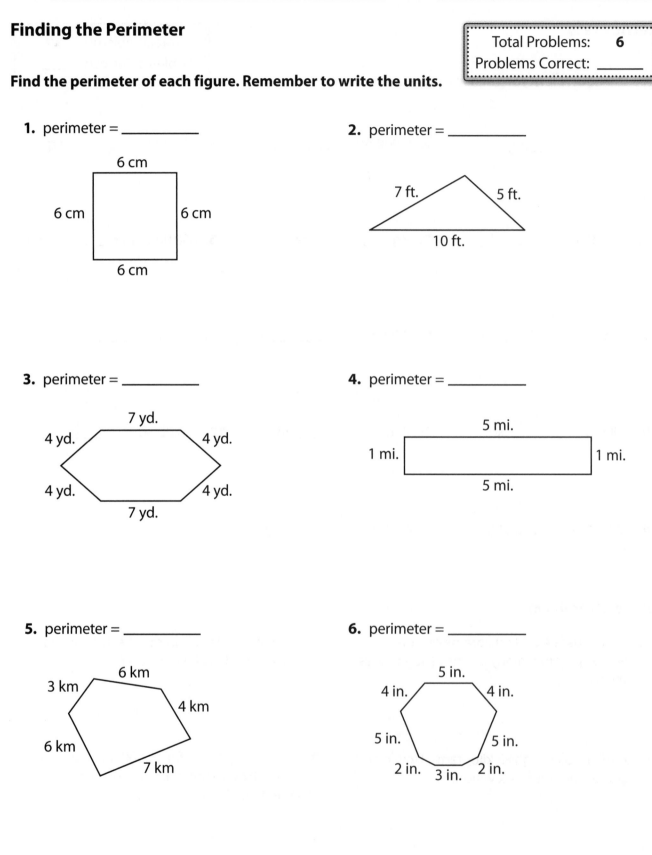

1. perimeter = _____

6 cm

6 cm   6 cm

6 cm

2. perimeter = _____

7 ft.   5 ft.

10 ft.

3. perimeter = _____

7 yd.

4 yd.   4 yd.

4 yd.   4 yd.

7 yd.

4. perimeter = _____

5 mi.

1 mi.   1 mi.

5 mi.

5. perimeter = _____

6 km

3 km

4 km

6 km

7 km

6. perimeter = _____

5 in.

4 in.   4 in.

5 in.   5 in.

2 in.   3 in.   2 in.

Name _____   Date _____

Finding the Area

Find the area of each figure. Remember to write the square (sq.) units.

1. area = _____

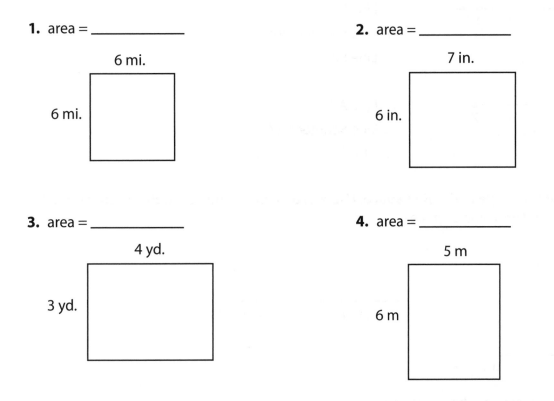

6 mi.

6 mi.

2. area = _____

7 in.

6 in.

3. area = _____

4 yd.

3 yd.

4. area = _____

5 m

6 m

Find the area of each quadrilateral with the given dimensions. Remember to write the square (sq.) units.

	Length	Width	Area
5.	10 in.	6 in.	
6.	5 cm	3 cm	
7.	4 yd.	3 yd.	
8.	10 km	4 km	
9.	4 mi.	4 mi.	
10.	6 ft.	3 ft.	

Geometry and Measurement Review

Circle the correct name for each line or line segment.

1.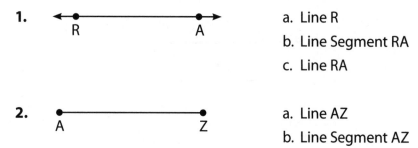
   a. Line R
   b. Line Segment RA
   c. Line RA

2.
   a. Line AZ
   b. Line Segment AZ
   c. Line Z

Write the name of the angle in the first space. Use a protractor to measure the angle and write the measurement in the second space.

3.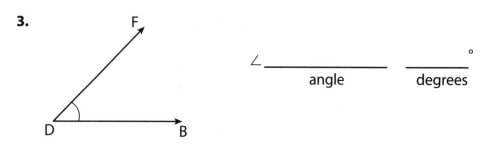

∠ _____ _____°
     angle   degrees

Label the circle according to the instructions.

4.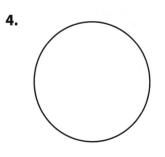

   a) Draw a point in the middle of the circle. Label it A.
   b) Draw a radius. Label it AB.
   c) Draw a diameter. Label it CD.
   d) Label the circle. Write the label above the circle.

Write the name of each figure in the blank.

5. 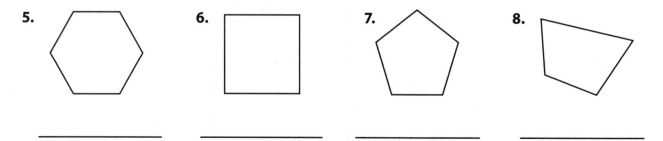 6. 7. 8.

_____ _____ _____ _____

Geometry and Measurement Review

```
╔══════════════════════════╗
║  Total Problems:    12    ║
║  Problems Correct: _____ ║
╚══════════════════════════╝
```

Circle the correct name for each figure.

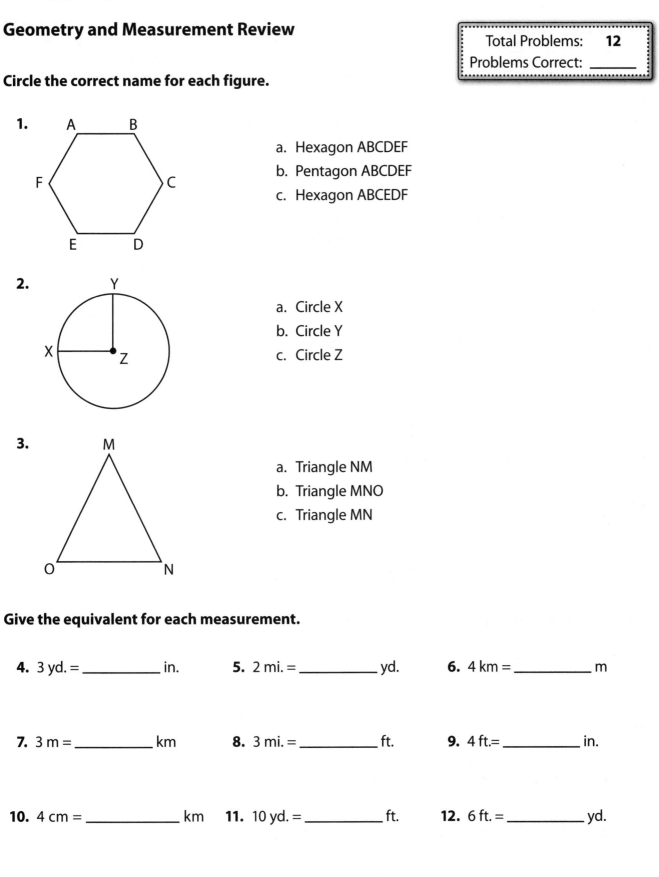

1.

   a. Hexagon ABCDEF

   b. Pentagon ABCDEF

   c. Hexagon ABCEDF

2.

   a. Circle X

   b. Circle Y

   c. Circle Z

3.

   a. Triangle NM

   b. Triangle MNO

   c. Triangle MN

Give the equivalent for each measurement.

4. 3 yd. = _____ in.

5. 2 mi. = _____ yd.

6. 4 km = _____ m

7. 3 m = _____ km

8. 3 mi. = _____ ft.

9. 4 ft.= _____ in.

10. 4 cm = _____ km

11. 10 yd. = _____ ft.

12. 6 ft. = _____ yd.

Cumulative Review

Solve each problem. Regroup when necessary.

1. $\begin{array}{r} 27 \\ + 52 \\ \hline \end{array}$

2. $\begin{array}{r} 325 \\ 415 \\ + 75 \\ \hline \end{array}$

3. $\begin{array}{r} 89 \\ + 74 \\ \hline \end{array}$

4. $\begin{array}{r} 7,254 \\ - 5,132 \\ \hline \end{array}$

5. $\begin{array}{r} 125 \\ + 367 \\ \hline \end{array}$

6. $\begin{array}{r} 4,015 \\ 3,922 \\ + 1,647 \\ \hline \end{array}$

7. $\begin{array}{r} 452 \\ - 49 \\ \hline \end{array}$

8. $\begin{array}{r} 6,025 \\ 4,098 \\ + 2,362 \\ \hline \end{array}$

9. $\begin{array}{r} 865 \\ - 72 \\ \hline \end{array}$

10. $\begin{array}{r} 5,094 \\ - 2,678 \\ \hline \end{array}$

11. $\begin{array}{r} 92 \\ \times 8 \\ \hline \end{array}$

12. $\begin{array}{r} 13 \\ \times 63 \\ \hline \end{array}$

13. $\begin{array}{r} 785 \\ \times 102 \\ \hline \end{array}$

14. $14\overline{)555}$

15. $37\overline{)6,721}$

16. $63 \times 52 =$

17. $85 \times 919 =$

18. $362 \div 12 =$

Write each fraction in simplest form.

19. $\dfrac{20}{30} =$

20. $\dfrac{24}{48} =$

21. $\dfrac{25}{75} =$

22. $\dfrac{10}{12} =$

23. $\dfrac{35}{140} =$

Write each improper fraction as a mixed number.

24. $\dfrac{8}{6} =$

25. $\dfrac{25}{10} =$

26. $\dfrac{51}{15} =$

27. $\dfrac{16}{9} =$

28. $\dfrac{120}{18} =$

Write each mixed number as an improper fraction.

29. $1\dfrac{2}{5} =$

30. $4\dfrac{3}{8} =$

31. $3\dfrac{2}{3} =$

32. $7\dfrac{5}{6} =$

Name _____   Date _____

Cumulative Review

Write the missing numerator to make each pair equivalent.

1. $\dfrac{1}{3} = \dfrac{}{18}$ 2. $\dfrac{6}{7} = \dfrac{}{42}$ 3. $\dfrac{9}{10} = \dfrac{}{50}$ 4. $\dfrac{3}{4} = \dfrac{}{20}$ 5. $\dfrac{3}{5} = \dfrac{}{25}$

Solve each problem. Write the answer in simplest form.

6. $\dfrac{3}{7} + \dfrac{2}{7} =$ 7. $\dfrac{1}{4} + \dfrac{4}{5} =$ 8. $\dfrac{6}{6} - \dfrac{3}{3} =$ 9. $\dfrac{15}{17} + \dfrac{16}{17} =$

10. $4\dfrac{1}{4} - 2\dfrac{3}{4} =$ 11. $3\dfrac{3}{9} + 4\dfrac{5}{18} =$ 12. $2\dfrac{2}{5} + 3\dfrac{3}{15} =$

Solve each problem. Write the answer in simplest form.

13. $\dfrac{5}{7} \times \dfrac{2}{7} =$ 14. $2 \times \dfrac{1}{3} =$ 15. $\dfrac{5}{8} \times \dfrac{3}{8} =$ 16. $\dfrac{1}{2} \times \dfrac{4}{5} =$

17. $4\dfrac{1}{4} \times 2\dfrac{3}{4} =$ 18. $2\dfrac{7}{8} \times 6\dfrac{2}{3} =$ 19. $2\dfrac{3}{5} \times 5\dfrac{1}{2} =$

Solve each problem. Regroup when necessary.

20. $\begin{array}{r} 3.1 \\ +\ 6.2 \\ \hline \end{array}$
21. $\begin{array}{r} 5.9 \\ +\ 4.2 \\ \hline \end{array}$
22. $\begin{array}{r} 74.06 \\ -\ 3.1 \\ \hline \end{array}$
23. $\begin{array}{r} 86.29 \\ +\ 0.03 \\ \hline \end{array}$
24. $\begin{array}{r} 406.34 \\ -\ 26.12 \\ \hline \end{array}$

25. $42.5 + 1.8 =$ 26. $13.1 + 5.5 =$

27. $34.23 + 16.5 =$ 28. $45.31 - 17.2 =$

Cumulative Review

Solve each problem.

1.　12
　　× 3.4

2.　23
　　× 0.16

3.　9.63
　　× 12.2

4.　0.953
　　×　0.7

5.　0.75
　　×　0.3

6. 5)18.5

7. 0.27)224.1

8. 8)25.6

9. 16)89.6

10. 121 × 1.2 =

11. 89.6 ÷ 16 =

12. 0.75 × 3 =

13. 0.996 ÷ 12 =

14. 0.721 ÷ 7 =

15. 0.50 ÷ 2 =

16. 2.84 × 16.5 =

17. 25.6 ÷ 8 =

18. 0.4 × 0.86 =

19. 30 ÷ 0.25 =

20. 10 ÷ 0.20 =

21. 70 ÷ 0.35 =

Cumulative Review

Total Problems: **19**
Problems Correct: _____

Write each decimal as a fraction in simplest form.

1. $5.2 =$ **2.** $0.5 =$ **3.** $6.8 =$ **4.** $2.52 =$ **5.** $12.36 =$

Write each fraction or mixed number as a decimal.

6. $\dfrac{1}{8} =$ **7.** $\dfrac{3}{4} =$ **8.** $2\dfrac{3}{8} =$ **9.** $5\dfrac{3}{4} =$ **10.** $3\dfrac{3}{5} =$

Draw and label the following.

11. Line QR   **12.** Line Segment AB

13. Angle MNO   **14.** Circle S with Radius ST

15. Hexagon HIJKLM   **16.** Triangle PQR

Give the equivalent for each measurement.

17. 1 ft. = _____ in.   **18.** 1 m = _____ km   **19.** 1 mi. = _____ yd.

Worksheet 1 (page 4)

Name _____ Date _____

Adding One- and Two-Digit Numbers

Solve each problem. Regroup when necessary.

Total Problems: **30**
Problems Correct: _____

1. 53 + 6 **59**	2. 25 + 5 **30**	3. 72 + 6 **78**	4. 22 + 6 **28**	5. 56 + 4 **60**	6. 14 + 9 **23**
7. 42 + 7 **49**	8. 17 + 9 **26**	9. 85 + 4 **89**	10. 45 + 3 **48**	11. 65 + 8 **73**	12. 38 + 6 **44**
13. 25 + 3 **28**	14. 10 + 2 **12**	15. 97 + 2 **99**	16. 69 + 8 **77**	17. 17 + 7 **24**	18. 51 + 7 **58**
19. 36 + 2 **38**	20. 49 + 8 **57**	21. 65 + 1 **66**	22. 72 + 4 **76**	23. 26 + 7 **33**	24. 62 + 4 **66**
25. 41 + 7 **48**	26. 65 + 9 **74**	27. 39 + 4 **43**	28. 87 + 9 **96**	29. 30 + 8 **38**	30. 43 + 5 **48**

Worksheet 2 (page 5)

Name _____ Date _____

Adding Two-Digit Numbers

Solve each problem. Regroup when necessary.

Total Problems: **30**
Problems Correct: _____

1. 36 + 54 **90**	2. 53 + 53 **106**	3. 12 + 24 **36**	4. 51 + 19 **70**	5. 28 + 27 **55**	6. 91 + 33 **124**
7. 42 + 17 **59**	8. 22 + 16 **38**	9. 60 + 32 **92**	10. 40 + 30 **70**	11. 53 + 10 **63**	12. 25 + 25 **50**
13. 85 + 12 **97**	14. 36 + 33 **69**	15. 48 + 72 **120**	16. 92 + 86 **178**	17. 43 + 21 **64**	18. 57 + 31 **88**
19. 99 + 27 **126**	20. 79 + 16 **95**	21. 63 + 49 **112**	22. 83 + 25 **108**	23. 78 + 65 **143**	24. 87 + 14 **101**
25. 25 + 15 **40**	26. 42 + 18 **60**	27. 89 + 11 **100**	28. 47 + 39 **86**	29. 90 + 62 **152**	30. 92 + 24 **116**

Worksheet 3 (page 6)

Name _____ Date _____

Adding Three- and Four-Digit Numbers

Solve each problem. Regroup when necessary.

Total Problems: **25**
Problems Correct: _____

1. 4,237 + 201 **4,438**	2. 9,841 + 520 **10,361**	3. 3,011 + 654 **3,665**	4. 4,472 + 689 **5,161**	5. 4,870 + 287 **5,157**
6. 5,968 + 525 **6,493**	7. 8,211 + 345 **8,556**	8. 8,432 + 137 **8,569**	9. 5,072 + 549 **5,621**	10. 6,580 + 871 **7,451**
11. 6,010 + 902 **6,912**	12. 9,076 + 153 **9,229**	13. 6,509 + 225 **6,734**	14. 2,389 + 422 **2,811**	15. 3,653 + 321 **3,974**
16. 7,546 + 561 **8,107**	17. 1,120 + 782 **1,902**	18. 6,029 + 367 **6,396**	19. 1,760 + 195 **1,955**	20. 4,661 + 128 **4,789**
21. 4,870 + 106 **4,976**	22. 2,436 + 618 **3,054**	23. 5,843 + 492 **6,335**	24. 7,352 + 254 **7,606**	25. 2,704 + 202 **2,906**

Worksheet 4 (page 7)

Name _____ Date _____

Adding Three- and Four-Digit Numbers

Solve each problem. Regroup when necessary.

Total Problems: **25**
Problems Correct: _____

1. 1,526 + 718 **2,244**	2. 3,804 + 207 **4,011**	3. 4,358 + 885 **5,243**	4. 5,145 + 788 **5,933**	5. 7,321 + 992 **8,313**
6. 4,159 + 936 **5,095**	7. 6,943 + 309 **7,252**	8. 6,200 + 356 **6,556**	9. 2,960 + 785 **3,745**	10. 2,635 + 223 **2,858**
11. 4,963 + 173 **5,136**	12. 2,488 + 395 **2,883**	13. 4,650 + 121 **4,771**	14. 4,540 + 124 **4,664**	15. 2,564 + 852 **3,416**
16. 6,879 + 316 **7,195**	17. 3,977 + 478 **4,455**	18. 2,456 + 522 **2,978**	19. 1,865 + 750 **2,615**	20. 3,245 + 321 **3,566**
21. 1,258 + 648 **1,906**	22. 2,655 + 165 **2,820**	23. 5,651 + 786 **6,437**	24. 6,441 + 230 **6,671**	25. 3,251 + 775 **4,026**

Worksheet 1 (page 8)

Name _____ Date _____

Three-Digit Column Addition

Total Problems: **25**
Problems Correct: _____

Solve each problem. Regroup when necessary.

1. 453 125 + 678 **1,256**	2. 143 225 + 336 **704**	3. 612 717 + 246 **1,575**	4. 818 529 332 + 106 **1,785**	5. 533 397 864 + 702 **2,496**

1. 453 125 + 678 = **1,256**
2. 143 225 + 336 = **704**
3. 612 717 + 246 = **1,575**
4. 818 529 332 + 106 = **1,785**
5. 533 397 864 + 702 = **2,496**

6. 987 642 + 325 = **1,954**
7. 942 787 + 527 = **2,256**
8. 240 135 + 167 = **542**
9. 954 623 873 + 480 = **2,930**
10. 405 612 935 + 360 = **2,312**

11. 202 169 + 584 = **955**
12. 609 333 + 175 = **1,117**
13. 892 357 + 418 = **1,667**
14. 987 789 102 + 201 = **2,079**
15. 220 115 780 + 650 = **1,765**

16. 376 825 + 916 = **2,117**
17. 210 422 + 871 = **1,503**
18. 275 245 + 106 = **626**
19. 123 497 675 + 542 = **1,837**
20. 771 860 550 + 137 = **2,318**

21. 500 627 + 220 = **1,347**
22. 904 409 + 105 = **1,418**
23. 318 771 + 522 = **1,611**
24. 901 801 710 + 410 = **2,822**
25. 147 257 662 + 770 = **1,836**

Worksheet 2 (page 9)

Name _____ Date _____

Multi-Digit Column Addition

Total Problems: **20**
Problems Correct: _____

Solve each problem. Regroup when necessary.

1. 2,671 406 125 + 52 = **3,254**
2. 7,732 806 325 + 54 = **8,917**
3. 5,306 525 24 + 92 = **5,947**
4. 8,214 248 200 + 17 = **8,679**
5. 3,850 403 35 + 16 = **4,304**

6. 6,210 5,332 407 + 15 = **11,964**
7. 2,591 2,624 106 + 33 = **5,354**
8. 9,200 408 146 + 3 = **9,757**
9. 2,560 17 62 + 54 = **2,693**
10. 3,275 3,902 7,340 + 803 = **15,320**

11. 4,305 307 34 + 67 = **4,713**
12. 3,084 192 764 + 26 = **4,066**
13. 8,430 217 2,560 + 32 = **11,239**
14. 3,243 8,395 731 + 43 = **12,412**
15. 9,876 1,445 324 + 225 = **11,870**

16. 4,321 403 809 + 21 = **5,554**
17. 621 503 97 + 7 = **1,228**
18. 6,035 532 172 + 63 = **6,802**
19. 3,298 867 144 + 54 = **4,363**
20. 9,210 726 50 + 4 = **9,990**

Worksheet 3 (page 10)

Name _____ Date _____

Subtracting One-Digit Numbers from Two-Digit Numbers

Total Problems: **30**
Problems Correct: _____

Solve each problem. Regroup when necessary.

1. 35 − 5 = **30**
2. 62 − 9 = **53**
3. 51 − 7 = **44**
4. 64 − 3 = **61**
5. 25 − 4 = **21**
6. 73 − 2 = **71**

7. 42 − 7 = **35**
8. 47 − 8 = **39**
9. 62 − 5 = **57**
10. 87 − 5 = **82**
11. 88 − 7 = **81**
12. 86 − 9 = **77**

13. 18 − 9 = **9**
14. 25 − 3 = **22**
15. 84 − 5 = **79**
16. 97 − 4 = **93**
17. 95 − 4 = **91**
18. 32 − 8 = **24**

19. 27 − 3 = **24**
20. 33 − 5 = **28**
21. 92 − 9 = **83**
22. 92 − 0 = **92**
23. 89 − 0 = **89**
24. 75 − 3 = **72**

25. 56 − 6 = **50**
26. 59 − 8 = **51**
27. 49 − 6 = **43**
28. 76 − 7 = **69**
29. 32 − 6 = **26**
30. 53 − 2 = **51**

Worksheet 4 (page 11)

Name _____ Date _____

Subtracting Multi-Digit Numbers

Total Problems: **25**
Problems Correct: _____

Solve each problem. Regroup when necessary.

1. 302 − 25 = **277**
2. 800 − 72 = **728**
3. 154 − 109 = **45**
4. 2,487 − 333 = **2,154**
5. 4,176 − 328 = **3,848**

6. 604 − 52 = **552**
7. 133 − 54 = **79**
8. 387 − 275 = **112**
9. 5,879 − 631 = **5,248**
10. 5,912 − 756 = **5,156**

11. 479 − 63 = **416**
12. 175 − 87 = **88**
13. 488 − 243 = **245**
14. 1,250 − 758 = **492**
15. 7,895 − 167 = **7,728**

16. 527 − 49 = **478**
17. 992 − 36 = **956**
18. 767 − 516 = **251**
19. 6,840 − 522 = **6,318**
20. 1,786 − 250 = **1,536**

21. 275 − 25 = **250**
22. 689 − 26 = **663**
23. 879 − 437 = **442**
24. 3,807 − 416 = **3,391**
25. 4,834 − 956 = **3,878**

Worksheet 1 (page 12)

Name _____ Date _____

Subtracting Multi-Digit Numbers

Solve each problem. Regroup when necessary.

Total Problems: 16
Problems Correct: _____

1. $\begin{array}{r} 30,821 \\ -\ 4,163 \\ \hline 26,658 \end{array}$
2. $\begin{array}{r} 72,541 \\ -\ 8,530 \\ \hline 64,011 \end{array}$
3. $\begin{array}{r} 44,785 \\ -\ 27,556 \\ \hline 17,229 \end{array}$
4. $\begin{array}{r} 42,165 \\ -\ 30,708 \\ \hline 11,457 \end{array}$

5. $\begin{array}{r} 52,964 \\ -\ 3,175 \\ \hline 49,789 \end{array}$
6. $\begin{array}{r} 76,283 \\ -\ 7,657 \\ \hline 68,626 \end{array}$
7. $\begin{array}{r} 35,463 \\ -\ 27,540 \\ \hline 7,923 \end{array}$
8. $\begin{array}{r} 40,081 \\ -\ 21,721 \\ \hline 18,360 \end{array}$

9. $\begin{array}{r} 87,576 \\ -\ 6,353 \\ \hline 81,223 \end{array}$
10. $\begin{array}{r} 94,443 \\ -\ 7,785 \\ \hline 86,658 \end{array}$
11. $\begin{array}{r} 46,724 \\ -\ 20,407 \\ \hline 26,317 \end{array}$
12. $\begin{array}{r} 31,621 \\ -\ 23,126 \\ \hline 8,495 \end{array}$

13. $\begin{array}{r} 83,542 \\ -\ 6,427 \\ \hline 77,115 \end{array}$
14. $\begin{array}{r} 62,083 \\ -\ 7,228 \\ \hline 54,855 \end{array}$
15. $\begin{array}{r} 72,450 \\ -\ 36,000 \\ \hline 36,450 \end{array}$
16. $\begin{array}{r} 92,140 \\ -\ 12,306 \\ \hline 79,834 \end{array}$

12 CD-104321 • © Carson-Dellosa

Worksheet 2 (page 13)

Name _____ Date _____

Multiplying One- and Two-Digit Numbers

Solve each problem. Regroup when necessary.

Total Problems: 30
Problems Correct: _____

1. $\begin{array}{r} 2 \\ \times 8 \\ \hline 16 \end{array}$
2. $\begin{array}{r} 8 \\ \times 8 \\ \hline 64 \end{array}$
3. $\begin{array}{r} 10 \\ \times 10 \\ \hline 100 \end{array}$
4. $\begin{array}{r} 7 \\ \times 7 \\ \hline 49 \end{array}$
5. $\begin{array}{r} 3 \\ \times 5 \\ \hline 15 \end{array}$
6. $\begin{array}{r} 12 \\ \times 4 \\ \hline 48 \end{array}$

7. $\begin{array}{r} 4 \\ \times 6 \\ \hline 24 \end{array}$
8. $\begin{array}{r} 3 \\ \times 7 \\ \hline 21 \end{array}$
9. $\begin{array}{r} 11 \\ \times 11 \\ \hline 121 \end{array}$
10. $\begin{array}{r} 6 \\ \times 6 \\ \hline 36 \end{array}$
11. $\begin{array}{r} 12 \\ \times 2 \\ \hline 24 \end{array}$
12. $\begin{array}{r} 6 \\ \times 9 \\ \hline 54 \end{array}$

13. $\begin{array}{r} 10 \\ \times 9 \\ \hline 90 \end{array}$
14. $\begin{array}{r} 4 \\ \times 8 \\ \hline 32 \end{array}$
15. $\begin{array}{r} 4 \\ \times 9 \\ \hline 36 \end{array}$
16. $\begin{array}{r} 5 \\ \times 5 \\ \hline 25 \end{array}$
17. $\begin{array}{r} 11 \\ \times 1 \\ \hline 11 \end{array}$
18. $\begin{array}{r} 15 \\ \times 2 \\ \hline 30 \end{array}$

19. $\begin{array}{r} 6 \\ \times 7 \\ \hline 42 \end{array}$
20. $\begin{array}{r} 9 \\ \times 5 \\ \hline 45 \end{array}$
21. $\begin{array}{r} 12 \\ \times 3 \\ \hline 36 \end{array}$
22. $\begin{array}{r} 3 \\ \times 4 \\ \hline 12 \end{array}$
23. $\begin{array}{r} 4 \\ \times 7 \\ \hline 28 \end{array}$
24. $\begin{array}{r} 13 \\ \times 3 \\ \hline 39 \end{array}$

25. $\begin{array}{r} 11 \\ \times 5 \\ \hline 55 \end{array}$
26. $\begin{array}{r} 3 \\ \times 9 \\ \hline 27 \end{array}$
27. $\begin{array}{r} 11 \\ \times 8 \\ \hline 88 \end{array}$
28. $\begin{array}{r} 10 \\ \times 2 \\ \hline 20 \end{array}$
29. $\begin{array}{r} 5 \\ \times 2 \\ \hline 10 \end{array}$
30. $\begin{array}{r} 18 \\ \times 1 \\ \hline 18 \end{array}$

CD-104321 • © Carson-Dellosa 13

Worksheet 3 (page 14)

Name _____ Date _____

Multiplying One- and Two-Digit Numbers

Solve each problem. Regroup when necessary.

Total Problems: 30
Problems Correct: _____

1. $\begin{array}{r} 12 \\ \times 12 \\ \hline 144 \end{array}$
2. $\begin{array}{r} 9 \\ \times 9 \\ \hline 81 \end{array}$
3. $\begin{array}{r} 2 \\ \times 9 \\ \hline 18 \end{array}$
4. $\begin{array}{r} 4 \\ \times 7 \\ \hline 28 \end{array}$
5. $\begin{array}{r} 11 \\ \times 3 \\ \hline 33 \end{array}$
6. $\begin{array}{r} 3 \\ \times 8 \\ \hline 24 \end{array}$

7. $\begin{array}{r} 12 \\ \times 4 \\ \hline 48 \end{array}$
8. $\begin{array}{r} 10 \\ \times 4 \\ \hline 40 \end{array}$
9. $\begin{array}{r} 10 \\ \times 3 \\ \hline 30 \end{array}$
10. $\begin{array}{r} 12 \\ \times 5 \\ \hline 60 \end{array}$
11. $\begin{array}{r} 4 \\ \times 5 \\ \hline 20 \end{array}$
12. $\begin{array}{r} 4 \\ \times 4 \\ \hline 16 \end{array}$

13. $\begin{array}{r} 3 \\ \times 6 \\ \hline 18 \end{array}$
14. $\begin{array}{r} 11 \\ \times 9 \\ \hline 99 \end{array}$
15. $\begin{array}{r} 8 \\ \times 9 \\ \hline 72 \end{array}$
16. $\begin{array}{r} 11 \\ \times 2 \\ \hline 22 \end{array}$
17. $\begin{array}{r} 12 \\ \times 11 \\ \hline 132 \end{array}$
18. $\begin{array}{r} 6 \\ \times 9 \\ \hline 54 \end{array}$

19. $\begin{array}{r} 9 \\ \times 6 \\ \hline 54 \end{array}$
20. $\begin{array}{r} 12 \\ \times 7 \\ \hline 84 \end{array}$
21. $\begin{array}{r} 10 \\ \times 6 \\ \hline 60 \end{array}$
22. $\begin{array}{r} 12 \\ \times 6 \\ \hline 72 \end{array}$
23. $\begin{array}{r} 12 \\ \times 10 \\ \hline 120 \end{array}$
24. $\begin{array}{r} 9 \\ \times 9 \\ \hline 81 \end{array}$

25. $\begin{array}{r} 11 \\ \times 7 \\ \hline 77 \end{array}$
26. $\begin{array}{r} 11 \\ \times 12 \\ \hline 132 \end{array}$
27. $\begin{array}{r} 10 \\ \times 11 \\ \hline 110 \end{array}$
28. $\begin{array}{r} 6 \\ \times 8 \\ \hline 48 \end{array}$
29. $\begin{array}{r} 10 \\ \times 5 \\ \hline 50 \end{array}$
30. $\begin{array}{r} 12 \\ \times 3 \\ \hline 36 \end{array}$

14 CD-104321 • © Carson-Dellosa

Worksheet 4 (page 15)

Name _____ Date _____

Multiplying One- and Two-Digit Numbers

Solve each problem. Regroup when necessary.

Total Problems: 30
Problems Correct: _____

1. $\begin{array}{r} 10 \\ \times 11 \\ \hline 110 \end{array}$
2. $\begin{array}{r} 10 \\ \times 7 \\ \hline 70 \end{array}$
3. $\begin{array}{r} 1 \\ \times 9 \\ \hline 9 \end{array}$
4. $\begin{array}{r} 3 \\ \times 7 \\ \hline 21 \end{array}$
5. $\begin{array}{r} 15 \\ \times 4 \\ \hline 60 \end{array}$
6. $\begin{array}{r} 1 \\ \times 8 \\ \hline 8 \end{array}$

7. $\begin{array}{r} 13 \\ \times 5 \\ \hline 65 \end{array}$
8. $\begin{array}{r} 11 \\ \times 5 \\ \hline 55 \end{array}$
9. $\begin{array}{r} 3 \\ \times 8 \\ \hline 24 \end{array}$
10. $\begin{array}{r} 11 \\ \times 4 \\ \hline 44 \end{array}$
11. $\begin{array}{r} 14 \\ \times 3 \\ \hline 42 \end{array}$
12. $\begin{array}{r} 2 \\ \times 4 \\ \hline 8 \end{array}$

13. $\begin{array}{r} 4 \\ \times 5 \\ \hline 20 \end{array}$
14. $\begin{array}{r} 10 \\ \times 6 \\ \hline 60 \end{array}$
15. $\begin{array}{r} 5 \\ \times 9 \\ \hline 45 \end{array}$
16. $\begin{array}{r} 10 \\ \times 3 \\ \hline 30 \end{array}$
17. $\begin{array}{r} 11 \\ \times 8 \\ \hline 88 \end{array}$
18. $\begin{array}{r} 3 \\ \times 9 \\ \hline 27 \end{array}$

19. $\begin{array}{r} 8 \\ \times 2 \\ \hline 16 \end{array}$
20. $\begin{array}{r} 10 \\ \times 4 \\ \hline 40 \end{array}$
21. $\begin{array}{r} 10 \\ \times 7 \\ \hline 70 \end{array}$
22. $\begin{array}{r} 12 \\ \times 1 \\ \hline 12 \end{array}$
23. $\begin{array}{r} 10 \\ \times 6 \\ \hline 60 \end{array}$
24. $\begin{array}{r} 9 \\ \times 8 \\ \hline 72 \end{array}$

25. $\begin{array}{r} 10 \\ \times 5 \\ \hline 50 \end{array}$
26. $\begin{array}{r} 17 \\ \times 12 \\ \hline 204 \end{array}$
27. $\begin{array}{r} 11 \\ \times 8 \\ \hline 88 \end{array}$
28. $\begin{array}{r} 2 \\ \times 8 \\ \hline 16 \end{array}$
29. $\begin{array}{r} 12 \\ \times 5 \\ \hline 60 \end{array}$
30. $\begin{array}{r} 1 \\ \times 4 \\ \hline 4 \end{array}$

CD-104321 • © Carson-Dellosa 15

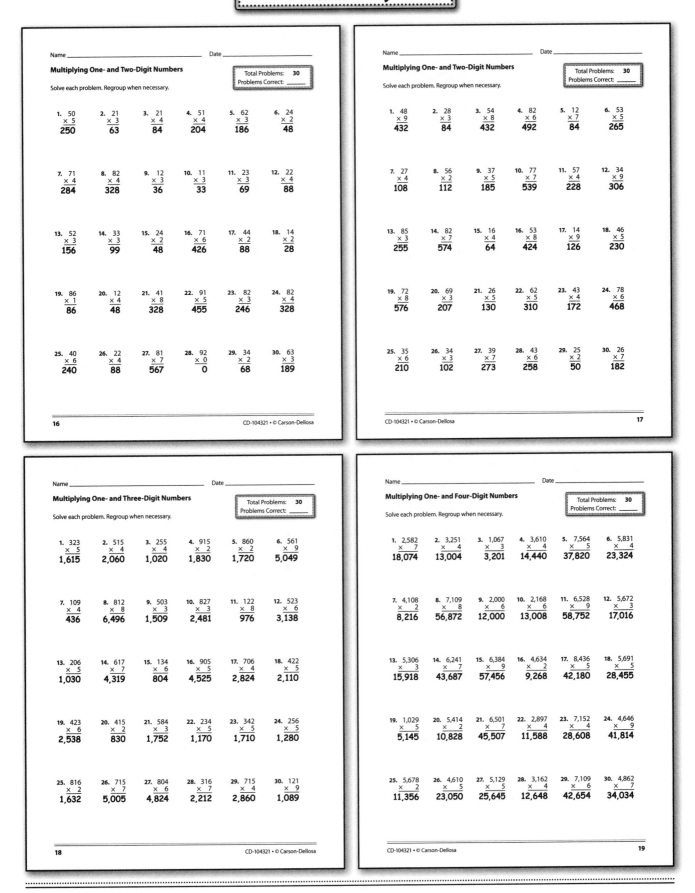

Name _____ **Date** _____

Multiplying One- and Two-Digit Numbers

Total Problems:	30
Problems Correct:	___

Solve each problem. Regroup when necessary.

1. 50 × 5 = **250**
2. 21 × 3 = **63**
3. 21 × 4 = **84**
4. 51 × 4 = **204**
5. 62 × 3 = **186**
6. 24 × 2 = **48**

7. 71 × 4 = **284**
8. 82 × 4 = **328**
9. 12 × 3 = **36**
10. 11 × 3 = **33**
11. 23 × 3 = **69**
12. 22 × 4 = **88**

13. 52 × 3 = **156**
14. 33 × 3 = **99**
15. 24 × 2 = **48**
16. 71 × 6 = **426**
17. 44 × 2 = **88**
18. 14 × 2 = **28**

19. 86 × 1 = **86**
20. 12 × 4 = **48**
21. 41 × 8 = **328**
22. 91 × 5 = **455**
23. 82 × 3 = **246**
24. 82 × 4 = **328**

25. 40 × 6 = **240**
26. 22 × 4 = **88**
27. 81 × 7 = **567**
28. 92 × 0 = **0**
29. 34 × 2 = **68**
30. 63 × 3 = **189**

16   CD-104321 • © Carson-Dellosa

Name _____ **Date** _____

Multiplying One- and Two-Digit Numbers

Total Problems:	30
Problems Correct:	___

Solve each problem. Regroup when necessary.

1. 48 × 9 = **432**
2. 28 × 3 = **84**
3. 54 × 8 = **432**
4. 82 × 6 = **492**
5. 12 × 7 = **84**
6. 53 × 5 = **265**

7. 27 × 4 = **108**
8. 56 × 2 = **112**
9. 37 × 5 = **185**
10. 77 × 7 = **539**
11. 57 × 4 = **228**
12. 34 × 9 = **306**

13. 85 × 3 = **255**
14. 82 × 7 = **574**
15. 16 × 4 = **64**
16. 53 × 8 = **424**
17. 14 × 9 = **126**
18. 46 × 5 = **230**

19. 72 × 8 = **576**
20. 69 × 3 = **207**
21. 26 × 5 = **130**
22. 62 × 5 = **310**
23. 43 × 4 = **172**
24. 78 × 6 = **468**

25. 35 × 6 = **210**
26. 34 × 3 = **102**
27. 39 × 7 = **273**
28. 43 × 6 = **258**
29. 25 × 2 = **50**
30. 26 × 7 = **182**

CD-104321 • © Carson-Dellosa   17

Name _____ **Date** _____

Multiplying One- and Three-Digit Numbers

Total Problems:	30
Problems Correct:	___

Solve each problem. Regroup when necessary.

1. 323 × 5 = **1,615**
2. 515 × 4 = **2,060**
3. 255 × 4 = **1,020**
4. 915 × 2 = **1,830**
5. 860 × 2 = **1,720**
6. 561 × 9 = **5,049**

7. 109 × 4 = **436**
8. 812 × 8 = **6,496**
9. 503 × 3 = **1,509**
10. 827 × 3 = **2,481**
11. 122 × 8 = **976**
12. 523 × 6 = **3,138**

13. 206 × 5 = **1,030**
14. 617 × 7 = **4,319**
15. 134 × 6 = **804**
16. 905 × 5 = **4,525**
17. 706 × 4 = **2,824**
18. 422 × 5 = **2,110**

19. 423 × 6 = **2,538**
20. 415 × 2 = **830**
21. 584 × 3 = **1,752**
22. 234 × 5 = **1,170**
23. 342 × 5 = **1,710**
24. 256 × 5 = **1,280**

25. 816 × 2 = **1,632**
26. 715 × 7 = **5,005**
27. 804 × 6 = **4,824**
28. 316 × 7 = **2,212**
29. 715 × 4 = **2,860**
30. 121 × 9 = **1,089**

18   CD-104321 • © Carson-Dellosa

Name _____ **Date** _____

Multiplying One- and Four-Digit Numbers

Total Problems:	30
Problems Correct:	___

Solve each problem. Regroup when necessary.

1. 2,582 × 7 = **18,074**
2. 3,251 × 4 = **13,004**
3. 1,067 × 3 = **3,201**
4. 3,610 × 4 = **14,440**
5. 7,564 × 5 = **37,820**
6. 5,831 × 4 = **23,324**

7. 4,108 × 2 = **8,216**
8. 7,109 × 8 = **56,872**
9. 2,000 × 6 = **12,000**
10. 2,168 × 6 = **13,008**
11. 6,528 × 9 = **58,752**
12. 5,672 × 3 = **17,016**

13. 5,306 × 3 = **15,918**
14. 6,241 × 7 = **43,687**
15. 6,384 × 9 = **57,456**
16. 4,634 × 2 = **9,268**
17. 8,436 × 5 = **42,180**
18. 5,691 × 5 = **28,455**

19. 1,029 × 5 = **5,145**
20. 5,414 × 2 = **10,828**
21. 6,501 × 7 = **45,507**
22. 2,897 × 4 = **11,588**
23. 7,152 × 4 = **28,608**
24. 4,646 × 9 = **41,814**

25. 5,678 × 2 = **11,356**
26. 4,610 × 5 = **23,050**
27. 5,129 × 5 = **25,645**
28. 3,162 × 4 = **12,648**
29. 7,109 × 6 = **42,654**
30. 4,862 × 7 = **34,034**

CD-104321 • © Carson-Dellosa   19

Worksheet 1 (page 20)

Name _____ Date _____

Multiplying Two-Digit Numbers

Solve each problem. Regroup when necessary.

Total Problems: 25
Problems Correct: _____

#	Problem	Answer
1.	41×18	738
2.	53×38	2,014
3.	73×46	3,358
4.	42×30	1,260
5.	86×75	6,450
6.	38×22	836
7.	36×12	432
8.	62×44	2,728
9.	81×72	5,832
10.	56×13	728
11.	64×47	3,008
12.	82×51	4,182
13.	25×17	425
14.	91×43	3,913
15.	49×28	1,372
16.	68×32	2,176
17.	42×18	756
18.	86×42	3,612
19.	35×28	980
20.	73×56	4,088
21.	72×43	3,096
22.	58×63	3,654
23.	83×27	2,241
24.	70×60	4,200
25.	54×27	1,458

Worksheet 2 (page 21)

Name _____ Date _____

Multiplying Two- and Three-Digit Numbers

Solve each problem. Regroup when necessary.

Total Problems: 25
Problems Correct: _____

#	Problem	Answer
1.	518×42	21,756
2.	216×10	2,160
3.	443×33	14,619
4.	687×51	35,037
5.	554×53	29,362
6.	729×56	40,824
7.	591×19	11,229
8.	248×75	18,600
9.	792×43	34,056
10.	456×14	6,384
11.	455×31	14,105
12.	327×35	11,445
13.	697×46	32,062
14.	826×26	21,476
15.	647×18	11,646
16.	512×60	30,720
17.	244×32	7,808
18.	843×12	10,116
19.	746×37	27,602
20.	535×79	42,265
21.	485×21	10,185
22.	123×45	5,535
23.	695×61	42,395
24.	792×49	38,808
25.	691×24	16,584

Worksheet 3 (page 22)

Name _____ Date _____

Multiplying Three-Digit Numbers

Solve each problem. Regroup when necessary.

Total Problems: 30
Problems Correct: _____

#	Problem	Answer
1.	654×189	123,606
2.	542×172	93,224
3.	323×247	79,781
4.	826×825	681,450
5.	340×285	96,900
6.	221×103	22,763
7.	365×184	67,160
8.	756×633	478,548
9.	236×420	99,120
10.	630×246	154,980
11.	416×122	50,752
12.	593×347	205,771
13.	724×377	272,948
14.	351×240	84,240
15.	577×290	167,330
16.	412×203	83,636
17.	593×347	205,771
18.	724×377	272,948
19.	251×141	35,391
20.	472×184	86,848
21.	350×491	171,850
22.	827×579	478,833
23.	520×397	206,440
24.	630×141	88,830
25.	770×143	110,110
26.	321×324	104,004
27.	427×273	116,571
28.	678×459	311,202
29.	517×510	263,670
30.	370×237	87,690

Worksheet 4 (page 23)

Name _____ Date _____

Division with One-Digit Quotients

Solve each problem.

Total Problems: 27
Problems Correct: _____

#	Problem	Answer
1.	$3\overline{)12}$	4
2.	$4\overline{)12}$	3
3.	$8\overline{)48}$	6
4.	$4\overline{)24}$	6
5.	$5\overline{)15}$	3
6.	$9\overline{)72}$	8
7.	$5\overline{)10}$	2
8.	$6\overline{)42}$	7
9.	$7\overline{)42}$	6
10.	$3\overline{)9}$	3
11.	$6\overline{)54}$	9
12.	$4\overline{)28}$	7
13.	$2\overline{)8}$	4
14.	$7\overline{)63}$	9
15.	$8\overline{)56}$	7
16.	$30 \div 5 =$	6
17.	$35 \div 7 =$	5
18.	$14 \div 7 =$	2
19.	$36 \div 9 =$	4
20.	$12 \div 6 =$	2
21.	$21 \div 7 =$	3
22.	$24 \div 6 =$	4
23.	$64 \div 8 =$	8
24.	$36 \div 9 =$	4
25.	$32 \div 4 =$	8
26.	$20 \div 5 =$	4
27.	$18 \div 6 =$	3

Name _____ Date _____

Division with Two-Digit Quotients

Total Problems: **30**
Problems Correct: _____

Solve each problem.

1. 6)72 = **12**   2. 5)90 = **18**   3. 3)93 = **31**

4. 2)36 = **18**   5. 3)96 = **32**   6. 3)66 = **22**

7. 7)98 = **14**   8. 4)72 = **18**   9. 7)91 = **13**

10. 4)40 = **10**   11. 7)84 = **12**   12. 6)78 = **13**

13. 3)36 = **12**   14. 7)70 = **10**   15. 8)88 = **11**

16. 5)55 = **11**   17. 5)90 = **18**   18. 5)95 = **19**

19. 2)24 = **12**   20. 6)84 = **14**   21. 9)99 = **11**

22. 3)81 = **27**   23. 3)75 = **25**   24. 3)51 = **17**

25. 8)80 = **10**   26. 2)86 = **43**   27. 4)96 = **24**

28. 3)45 = **15**   29. 5)85 = **17**   30. 8)80 = **10**

24   CD-104321 • © Carson-Dellosa

Name _____ Date _____

Division with Three-Digit Quotients

Total Problems: **20**
Problems Correct: _____

Solve each problem.

1. 9)1,368 = **152**   2. 4)1,228 = **307**   3. 8)5,392 = **674**   4. 6)1,878 = **313**

5. 5)1,395 = **279**   6. 7)2,926 = **418**   7. 4)1,008 = **252**   8. 5)975 = **195**

9. 4)2,128 = **532**   10. 2)1,224 = **612**   11. 6)2,706 = **451**   12. 3)2,019 = **673**

13. 3)1,008 = **336**   14. 8)3,888 = **486**   15. 7)1,421 = **203**   16. 5)1,125 = **225**

17. 2)1,024 = **512**   18. 3)1,134 = **378**   19. 8)4,960 = **620**   20. 9)2,790 = **310**

CD-104321 • © Carson-Dellosa   25

Name _____ Date _____

Division with One- and Two-Digit Quotients and Remainders

Total Problems: **27**
Problems Correct: _____

Solve each problem.

1. 7)82 = **11 r5**   2. 4)54 = **13 r2**   3. 3)26 = **8 r2**

4. 8)95 = **11 r7**   5. 4)18 = **4 r2**   6. 7)57 = **8 r1**

7. 4)63 = **15 r3**   8. 5)22 = **4 r2**   9. 5)18 = **3 r3**

10. 5)81 = **16 r1**   11. 4)41 = **10 r1**   12. 3)29 = **9 r2**

13. 6)74 = **12 r2**   14. 8)37 = **4 r5**   15. 5)42 = **8 r2**

16. 23 ÷ 5 = **4 r3**   17. 58 ÷ 7 = **8 r2**   18. 46 ÷ 5 = **9 r1**

19. 24 ÷ 7 = **3 r3**   20. 45 ÷ 6 = **7 r3**   21. 51 ÷ 7 = **7 r2**

22. 32 ÷ 6 = **5 r2**   23. 26 ÷ 3 = **8 r2**   24. 25 ÷ 4 = **6 r1**

25. 43 ÷ 2 = **21 r1**   26. 19 ÷ 2 = **9 r1**   27. 87 ÷ 9 = **9 r6**

26   CD-104321 • © Carson-Dellosa

Name _____ Date _____

Division with Two-Digit Quotients and Remainders

Total Problems: **30**
Problems Correct: _____

Solve each problem.

1. 6)82 = **13 r4**   2. 2)39 = **19 r1**   3. 8)89 = **11 r1**

4. 4)85 = **21 r1**   5. 4)70 = **17 r2**   6. 7)93 = **13 r2**

7. 3)59 = **19 r2**   8. 6)82 = **13 r4**   9. 2)81 = **40 r1**

10. 2)23 = **11 r1**   11. 8)94 = **11 r6**   12. 5)82 = **16 r2**

13. 4)97 = **24 r1**   14. 8)97 = **12 r1**   15. 7)92 = **13 r1**

16. 7)79 = **11 r2**   17. 5)79 = **15 r4**   18. 6)89 = **14 r5**

19. 5)63 = **12 r3**   20. 6)83 = **13 r5**   21. 7)81 = **11 r4**

22. 6)85 = **14 r1**   23. 6)89 = **14 r5**   24. 9)98 = **10 r8**

25. 3)67 = **22 r1**   26. 5)63 = **12 r3**   27. 6)73 = **12 r1**

28. 3)83 = **27 r2**   29. 7)85 = **12 r1**   30. 3)47 = **15 r2**

CD-104321 • © Carson-Dellosa   27

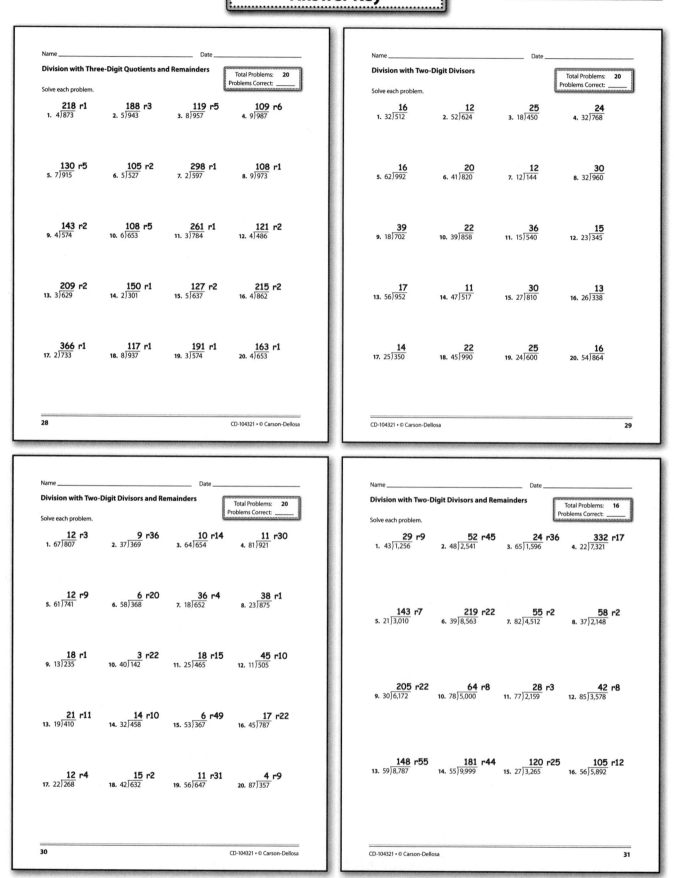

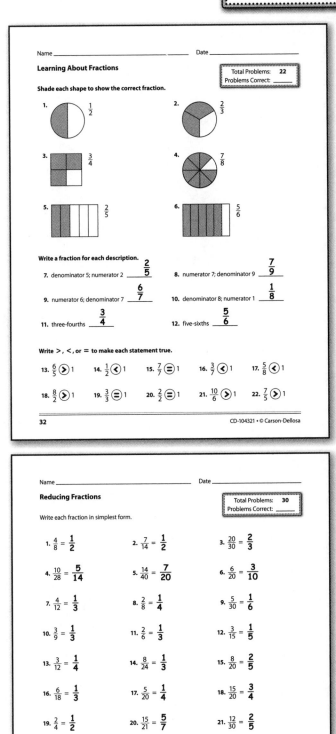

Name _____ **Date** _____

Learning About Fractions

Total Problems:	22
Problems Correct:	_____

Shade each shape to show the correct fraction.

1. $\frac{1}{2}$ 2. $\frac{2}{3}$

3. $\frac{3}{4}$ 4. $\frac{7}{8}$

5. $\frac{2}{5}$ 6. $\frac{5}{6}$

Write a fraction for each description.

7. denominator 5; numerator 2 $\frac{2}{5}$

8. numerator 7; denominator 9 $\frac{7}{9}$

9. numerator 6; denominator 7 $\frac{6}{7}$

10. denominator 8; numerator 1 $\frac{1}{8}$

11. three-fourths $\frac{3}{4}$

12. five-sixths $\frac{5}{6}$

Write >, <, or = to make each statement true.

13. $\frac{6}{5}$ (>) 1   14. $\frac{1}{2}$ (<) 1   15. $\frac{7}{7}$ (=) 1   16. $\frac{3}{7}$ (<) 1   17. $\frac{5}{8}$ (<) 1

18. $\frac{8}{2}$ (>) 1   19. $\frac{3}{3}$ (=) 1   20. $\frac{2}{2}$ (=) 1   21. $\frac{10}{6}$ (>) 1   22. $\frac{7}{5}$ (>) 1

CD-104321 • © Carson-Dellosa

Name _____ **Date** _____

Reducing Fractions

Total Problems:	30
Problems Correct:	_____

Write each fraction in simplest form.

1. $\frac{6}{8} = \frac{3}{4}$ 2. $\frac{3}{24} = \frac{1}{8}$ 3. $\frac{20}{35} = \frac{4}{7}$

4. $\frac{15}{20} = \frac{3}{4}$ 5. $\frac{10}{20} = \frac{1}{2}$ 6. $\frac{6}{16} = \frac{3}{8}$

7. $\frac{5}{20} = \frac{1}{4}$ 8. $\frac{4}{8} = \frac{1}{2}$ 9. $\frac{4}{16} = \frac{1}{4}$

10. $\frac{6}{9} = \frac{2}{3}$ 11. $\frac{4}{20} = \frac{1}{5}$ 12. $\frac{3}{15} = \frac{1}{5}$

13. $\frac{3}{12} = \frac{1}{4}$ 14. $\frac{5}{15} = \frac{1}{3}$ 15. $\frac{8}{16} = \frac{1}{2}$

16. $\frac{7}{21} = \frac{1}{3}$ 17. $\frac{5}{25} = \frac{1}{5}$ 18. $\frac{15}{30} = \frac{1}{2}$

19. $\frac{2}{8} = \frac{1}{4}$ 20. $\frac{14}{21} = \frac{2}{3}$ 21. $\frac{12}{16} = \frac{3}{4}$

22. $\frac{16}{32} = \frac{1}{2}$ 23. $\frac{7}{35} = \frac{1}{5}$ 24. $\frac{20}{40} = \frac{1}{2}$

25. $\frac{17}{34} = \frac{1}{2}$ 26. $\frac{10}{12} = \frac{5}{6}$ 27. $\frac{16}{24} = \frac{2}{3}$

28. $\frac{6}{18} = \frac{1}{3}$ 29. $\frac{5}{10} = \frac{1}{2}$ 30. $\frac{24}{32} = \frac{3}{4}$

CD-104321 • © Carson-Dellosa

Name _____ **Date** _____

Reducing Fractions

Total Problems:	30
Problems Correct:	_____

Write each fraction in simplest form.

1. $\frac{4}{8} = \frac{1}{2}$ 2. $\frac{7}{14} = \frac{1}{2}$ 3. $\frac{20}{30} = \frac{2}{3}$

4. $\frac{10}{28} = \frac{5}{14}$ 5. $\frac{14}{40} = \frac{7}{20}$ 6. $\frac{6}{20} = \frac{3}{10}$

7. $\frac{4}{12} = \frac{1}{3}$ 8. $\frac{2}{8} = \frac{1}{4}$ 9. $\frac{5}{30} = \frac{1}{6}$

10. $\frac{3}{9} = \frac{1}{3}$ 11. $\frac{2}{6} = \frac{1}{3}$ 12. $\frac{3}{15} = \frac{1}{5}$

13. $\frac{3}{12} = \frac{1}{4}$ 14. $\frac{8}{24} = \frac{1}{3}$ 15. $\frac{8}{20} = \frac{2}{5}$

16. $\frac{6}{18} = \frac{1}{3}$ 17. $\frac{5}{20} = \frac{1}{4}$ 18. $\frac{15}{20} = \frac{3}{4}$

19. $\frac{2}{4} = \frac{1}{2}$ 20. $\frac{15}{21} = \frac{5}{7}$ 21. $\frac{12}{30} = \frac{2}{5}$

22. $\frac{20}{22} = \frac{10}{11}$ 23. $\frac{7}{28} = \frac{1}{4}$ 24. $\frac{16}{32} = \frac{1}{2}$

25. $\frac{12}{15} = \frac{4}{5}$ 26. $\frac{18}{24} = \frac{3}{4}$ 27. $\frac{4}{18} = \frac{2}{9}$

28. $\frac{5}{15} = \frac{1}{3}$ 29. $\frac{15}{20} = \frac{3}{4}$ 30. $\frac{21}{45} = \frac{7}{15}$

CD-104321 • © Carson-Dellosa

Name _____ **Date** _____

Comparing Fractions

Total Problems:	21
Problems Correct:	_____

Write >, <, or = to make each statement true.

1. $\frac{16}{52}$ (<) $\frac{16}{25}$ 2. $\frac{13}{21}$ (<) $\frac{10}{13}$ 3. $\frac{16}{20}$ (>) $\frac{10}{25}$

4. $\frac{12}{32}$ (<) $\frac{12}{24}$ 5. $\frac{14}{16}$ (>) $\frac{15}{20}$ 6. $\frac{56}{88}$ (>) $\frac{25}{55}$

7. $\frac{16}{16}$ (=) $\frac{25}{25}$ 8. $\frac{4}{5}$ (<) $\frac{5}{6}$ 9. $\frac{9}{10}$ (>) $\frac{8}{15}$

10. $\frac{12}{24}$ (=) $\frac{2}{4}$ 11. $\frac{9}{15}$ (>) $\frac{4}{10}$ 12. $\frac{6}{15}$ (>) $\frac{4}{20}$

13. $\frac{16}{36}$ (<) $\frac{24}{27}$ 14. $\frac{25}{30}$ (>) $\frac{3}{18}$ 15. $\frac{7}{8}$ (>) $\frac{5}{9}$

16. $\frac{1}{2}$ (>) $\frac{24}{50}$ 17. $\frac{18}{21}$ (>) $\frac{12}{28}$ 18. $\frac{9}{12}$ (=) $\frac{15}{20}$

19. $\frac{35}{39}$ (>) $\frac{14}{24}$ 20. $\frac{16}{24}$ (=) $\frac{20}{30}$ 21. $\frac{21}{35}$ (<) $\frac{16}{24}$

CD-104321 • © Carson-Dellosa

Worksheet 1 (page 36)

Writing Improper Fractions as Mixed Numbers

Name _____ Date _____

Total Problems: **30**
Problems Correct: _____

Write each improper fraction as a mixed number in simplest form.

1. $\frac{4}{3} = 1\frac{1}{3}$ 2. $\frac{20}{15} = 1\frac{1}{3}$ 3. $\frac{7}{4} = 1\frac{3}{4}$

4. $\frac{55}{12} = 4\frac{7}{12}$ 5. $\frac{18}{5} = 3\frac{3}{5}$ 6. $\frac{5}{2} = 2\frac{1}{2}$

7. $\frac{5}{3} = 1\frac{2}{3}$ 8. $\frac{12}{5} = 2\frac{2}{5}$ 9. $\frac{13}{4} = 3\frac{1}{4}$

10. $\frac{15}{6} = 2\frac{1}{2}$ 11. $\frac{13}{2} = 6\frac{1}{2}$ 12. $\frac{17}{9} = 1\frac{8}{9}$

13. $\frac{10}{4} = 2\frac{1}{2}$ 14. $\frac{19}{2} = 9\frac{1}{2}$ 15. $\frac{27}{5} = 5\frac{2}{5}$

16. $\frac{15}{4} = 3\frac{3}{4}$ 17. $\frac{8}{3} = 2\frac{2}{3}$ 18. $\frac{15}{8} = 1\frac{7}{8}$

19. $\frac{6}{4} = 1\frac{1}{2}$ 20. $\frac{43}{7} = 6\frac{1}{7}$ 21. $\frac{19}{11} = 1\frac{8}{11}$

22. $\frac{20}{7} = 2\frac{6}{7}$ 23. $\frac{9}{4} = 2\frac{1}{4}$ 24. $\frac{17}{4} = 4\frac{1}{4}$

25. $\frac{10}{3} = 3\frac{1}{3}$ 26. $\frac{24}{10} = 2\frac{2}{5}$ 27. $\frac{9}{8} = 1\frac{1}{8}$

28. $\frac{16}{3} = 5\frac{1}{3}$ 29. $\frac{10}{3} = 3\frac{1}{3}$ 30. $\frac{50}{6} = 8\frac{1}{3}$

36   CD-104321 • © Carson-Dellosa

Worksheet 2 (page 37)

Writing Improper Fractions as Mixed Numbers

Name _____ Date _____

Total Problems: **30**
Problems Correct: _____

Write each improper fraction as a mixed number in simplest form.

1. $\frac{6}{4} = 1\frac{1}{2}$ 2. $\frac{21}{12} = 1\frac{3}{4}$ 3. $\frac{9}{4} = 2\frac{1}{4}$

4. $\frac{25}{11} = 2\frac{3}{11}$ 5. $\frac{19}{5} = 3\frac{4}{5}$ 6. $\frac{3}{2} = 1\frac{1}{2}$

7. $\frac{7}{4} = 1\frac{3}{4}$ 8. $\frac{13}{3} = 4\frac{1}{3}$ 9. $\frac{14}{6} = 2\frac{1}{3}$

10. $\frac{16}{5} = 3\frac{1}{5}$ 11. $\frac{13}{5} = 2\frac{3}{5}$ 12. $\frac{14}{8} = 1\frac{3}{4}$

13. $\frac{11}{2} = 5\frac{1}{2}$ 14. $\frac{17}{4} = 4\frac{1}{4}$ 15. $\frac{19}{2} = 9\frac{1}{2}$

16. $\frac{25}{3} = 8\frac{1}{3}$ 17. $\frac{8}{3} = 2\frac{2}{3}$ 18. $\frac{11}{6} = 1\frac{5}{6}$

19. $\frac{10}{3} = 3\frac{1}{3}$ 20. $\frac{33}{6} = 5\frac{1}{2}$ 21. $\frac{14}{9} = 1\frac{5}{9}$

22. $\frac{21}{8} = 2\frac{5}{8}$ 23. $\frac{7}{4} = 1\frac{3}{4}$ 24. $\frac{13}{3} = 4\frac{1}{3}$

25. $\frac{12}{5} = 2\frac{2}{5}$ 26. $\frac{18}{11} = 1\frac{7}{11}$ 27. $\frac{9}{2} = 4\frac{1}{2}$

28. $\frac{15}{4} = 3\frac{3}{4}$ 29. $\frac{10}{6} = 1\frac{2}{3}$ 30. $\frac{10}{4} = 2\frac{1}{2}$

CD-104321 • © Carson-Dellosa   37

Worksheet 3 (page 38)

Writing Improper Fractions as Mixed Numbers

Name _____ Date _____

Total Problems: **30**
Problems Correct: _____

Write each improper fraction as a mixed number in simplest form.

1. $\frac{9}{2} = 4\frac{1}{2}$ 2. $\frac{51}{10} = 5\frac{1}{10}$ 3. $\frac{19}{5} = 3\frac{4}{5}$

4. $\frac{8}{7} = 1\frac{1}{7}$ 5. $\frac{14}{13} = 1\frac{1}{13}$ 6. $\frac{8}{5} = 1\frac{3}{5}$

7. $\frac{12}{5} = 2\frac{2}{5}$ 8. $\frac{13}{7} = 1\frac{6}{7}$ 9. $\frac{16}{9} = 1\frac{7}{9}$

10. $\frac{10}{6} = 1\frac{2}{3}$ 11. $\frac{17}{7} = 2\frac{3}{7}$ 12. $\frac{13}{11} = 1\frac{2}{11}$

13. $\frac{11}{2} = 5\frac{1}{2}$ 14. $\frac{17}{6} = 2\frac{5}{6}$ 15. $\frac{25}{8} = 3\frac{1}{8}$

16. $\frac{11}{10} = 1\frac{1}{10}$ 17. $\frac{19}{18} = 1\frac{1}{18}$ 18. $\frac{26}{22} = 1\frac{2}{11}$

19. $\frac{16}{3} = 5\frac{1}{3}$ 20. $\frac{12}{5} = 2\frac{2}{5}$ 21. $\frac{3}{2} = 1\frac{1}{2}$

22. $\frac{61}{3} = 20\frac{1}{3}$ 23. $\frac{13}{12} = 1\frac{1}{12}$ 24. $\frac{47}{13} = 3\frac{8}{13}$

25. $\frac{11}{5} = 2\frac{1}{5}$ 26. $\frac{15}{14} = 1\frac{1}{14}$ 27. $\frac{6}{5} = 1\frac{1}{5}$

28. $\frac{15}{13} = 1\frac{2}{13}$ 29. $\frac{19}{11} = 1\frac{8}{11}$ 30. $\frac{10}{9} = 1\frac{1}{9}$

38   CD-104321 • © Carson-Dellosa

Worksheet 4 (page 39)

Writing Improper Fractions as Mixed Numbers

Name _____ Date _____

Total Problems: **30**
Problems Correct: _____

Write each improper fraction as a mixed number in simplest form.

1. $\frac{23}{15} = 1\frac{8}{15}$ 2. $\frac{40}{24} = 1\frac{2}{3}$ 3. $\frac{97}{33} = 2\frac{31}{33}$

4. $\frac{55}{12} = 4\frac{7}{12}$ 5. $\frac{26}{12} = 2\frac{1}{6}$ 6. $\frac{36}{34} = 1\frac{1}{17}$

7. $\frac{32}{15} = 2\frac{2}{15}$ 8. $\frac{89}{17} = 5\frac{4}{17}$ 9. $\frac{26}{15} = 1\frac{11}{15}$

10. $\frac{13}{4} = 3\frac{1}{4}$ 11. $\frac{59}{25} = 2\frac{9}{25}$ 12. $\frac{10}{8} = 1\frac{1}{4}$

13. $\frac{48}{5} = 9\frac{3}{5}$ 14. $\frac{66}{50} = 1\frac{8}{25}$ 15. $\frac{13}{3} = 4\frac{1}{3}$

16. $\frac{15}{4} = 3\frac{3}{4}$ 17. $\frac{6}{4} = 1\frac{1}{2}$ 18. $\frac{64}{49} = 1\frac{15}{49}$

19. $\frac{26}{4} = 6\frac{1}{2}$ 20. $\frac{44}{16} = 2\frac{3}{4}$ 21. $\frac{24}{20} = 1\frac{1}{5}$

22. $\frac{20}{7} = 2\frac{6}{7}$ 23. $\frac{17}{6} = 2\frac{5}{6}$ 24. $\frac{56}{11} = 5\frac{1}{11}$

25. $\frac{29}{7} = 4\frac{1}{7}$ 26. $\frac{62}{9} = 6\frac{8}{9}$ 27. $\frac{8}{3} = 2\frac{2}{3}$

28. $\frac{16}{3} = 5\frac{1}{3}$ 29. $\frac{20}{8} = 2\frac{1}{2}$ 30. $\frac{35}{12} = 2\frac{11}{12}$

CD-104321 • © Carson-Dellosa   39

Worksheet 1 (page 40)

Name _____ Date _____

Writing Mixed Numbers as Improper Fractions

Total Problems: 21
Problems Correct: _____

Write each mixed number as an improper fraction.

1. $3\frac{1}{2} = \frac{7}{2}$

2. $5\frac{7}{8} = \frac{47}{8}$

3. $7\frac{4}{5} = \frac{39}{5}$

4. $1\frac{1}{10} = \frac{11}{10}$

5. $6\frac{5}{8} = \frac{53}{8}$

6. $5\frac{2}{3} = \frac{17}{3}$

7. $9\frac{1}{2} = \frac{19}{2}$

8. $4\frac{3}{8} = \frac{35}{8}$

9. $8\frac{2}{3} = \frac{26}{3}$

10. $2\frac{2}{3} = \frac{8}{3}$

11. $2\frac{4}{9} = \frac{22}{9}$

12. $4\frac{3}{4} = \frac{19}{4}$

13. $2\frac{3}{8} = \frac{19}{8}$

14. $4\frac{2}{4} = \frac{18}{4}$

15. $6\frac{5}{7} = \frac{47}{7}$

16. $10\frac{3}{5} = \frac{53}{5}$

17. $4\frac{5}{9} = \frac{41}{9}$

18. $12\frac{13}{15} = \frac{193}{15}$

19. $3\frac{1}{3} = \frac{10}{3}$

20. $4\frac{2}{3} = \frac{14}{3}$

21. $6\frac{1}{5} = \frac{31}{5}$

40 CD-104321 • © Carson-Dellosa

Worksheet 2 (page 41)

Name _____ Date _____

Writing Mixed Numbers as Improper Fractions

Total Problems: 21
Problems Correct: _____

Write each mixed number as an improper fraction.

1. $1\frac{2}{3} = \frac{5}{3}$

2. $10\frac{5}{6} = \frac{65}{6}$

3. $5\frac{4}{5} = \frac{29}{5}$

4. $2\frac{1}{12} = \frac{25}{12}$

5. $12\frac{4}{5} = \frac{64}{5}$

6. $1\frac{1}{5} = \frac{6}{5}$

7. $7\frac{1}{6} = \frac{43}{6}$

8. $9\frac{6}{8} = \frac{78}{8}$

9. $9\frac{2}{8} = \frac{74}{8}$

10. $20\frac{2}{8} = \frac{162}{8}$

11. $8\frac{3}{9} = \frac{75}{9}$

12. $3\frac{3}{8} = \frac{27}{8}$

13. $2\frac{3}{4} = \frac{11}{4}$

14. $1\frac{1}{4} = \frac{5}{4}$

15. $15\frac{3}{4} = \frac{63}{4}$

16. $7\frac{10}{16} = \frac{122}{16}$

17. $11\frac{3}{9} = \frac{102}{9}$

18. $7\frac{5}{6} = \frac{47}{6}$

19. $3\frac{2}{5} = \frac{17}{5}$

20. $6\frac{1}{3} = \frac{19}{3}$

21. $7\frac{2}{5} = \frac{37}{5}$

CD-104321 • © Carson-Dellosa 41

Worksheet 3 (page 42)

Name _____ Date _____

Making Fractions Equivalent

Total Problems: 24
Problems Correct: _____

Write the missing numerator to make each pair equivalent.

1. $\frac{2}{3} = \frac{8}{12}$

2. $\frac{8}{9} = \frac{48}{54}$

3. $\frac{1}{2} = \frac{5}{10}$

4. $\frac{1}{8} = \frac{4}{32}$

5. $\frac{4}{9} = \frac{36}{81}$

6. $\frac{2}{9} = \frac{4}{18}$

7. $\frac{3}{4} = \frac{12}{16}$

8. $\frac{1}{2} = \frac{6}{12}$

9. $\frac{4}{5} = \frac{20}{25}$

10. $\frac{2}{5} = \frac{12}{30}$

11. $\frac{7}{8} = \frac{56}{64}$

12. $\frac{2}{3} = \frac{10}{15}$

13. $\frac{2}{5} = \frac{4}{10}$

14. $\frac{3}{8} = \frac{6}{16}$

15. $\frac{5}{8} = \frac{15}{24}$

16. $\frac{3}{4} = \frac{18}{24}$

17. $\frac{3}{5} = \frac{9}{15}$

18. $\frac{3}{7} = \frac{6}{14}$

19. $\frac{1}{6} = \frac{2}{12}$

20. $\frac{4}{5} = \frac{16}{20}$

21. $\frac{3}{7} = \frac{9}{21}$

22. $\frac{5}{6} = \frac{35}{42}$

23. $\frac{1}{6} = \frac{6}{36}$

24. $\frac{5}{8} = \frac{25}{40}$

42 CD-104321 • © Carson-Dellosa

Worksheet 4 (page 43)

Name _____ Date _____

Making Fractions Equivalent

Total Problems: 8
Problems Correct: _____

Write the missing numerators to make the fractions in each row equivalent.

1. $\frac{1}{2} = \frac{18}{36} = \frac{9}{18} = \frac{8}{16} = \frac{21}{42} = \frac{24}{48}$

2. $\frac{5}{6} = \frac{40}{48} = \frac{10}{12} = \frac{25}{30} = \frac{15}{18} = \frac{20}{24}$

3. $\frac{1}{3} = \frac{3}{9} = \frac{9}{27} = \frac{30}{90} = \frac{2}{6} = \frac{4}{12}$

4. $\frac{3}{4} = \frac{18}{24} = \frac{12}{16} = \frac{6}{8} = \frac{15}{20} = \frac{27}{36}$

5. $\frac{4}{9} = \frac{8}{18} = \frac{20}{45} = \frac{16}{36} = \frac{24}{54} = \frac{12}{27}$

6. $\frac{7}{8} = \frac{14}{16} = \frac{49}{56} = \frac{21}{24} = \frac{42}{48} = \frac{28}{32}$

7. $\frac{3}{7} = \frac{9}{21} = \frac{18}{42} = \frac{6}{14} = \frac{15}{35} = \frac{12}{28}$

8. $\frac{2}{5} = \frac{20}{50} = \frac{4}{10} = \frac{16}{40} = \frac{6}{15} = \frac{10}{25}$

CD-104321 • © Carson-Dellosa 43

Making Fractions Equivalent

Name _____ Date _____

Total Problems: **24**
Problems Correct: _____

Write the missing numerator to make each pair equivalent.

1. $4 = \dfrac{12}{3}$ 2. $6 = \dfrac{30}{5}$ 3. $\dfrac{2}{3} = \dfrac{12}{18}$

4. $\dfrac{1}{5} = \dfrac{4}{20}$ 5. $\dfrac{5}{6} = \dfrac{40}{48}$ 6. $\dfrac{1}{6} = \dfrac{6}{36}$

7. $\dfrac{1}{2} = \dfrac{4}{8}$ 8. $4 = \dfrac{8}{2}$ 9. $3 = \dfrac{6}{2}$

10. $\dfrac{5}{8} = \dfrac{25}{40}$ 11. $\dfrac{1}{3} = \dfrac{12}{36}$ 12. $\dfrac{2}{7} = \dfrac{14}{49}$

13. $\dfrac{1}{3} = \dfrac{2}{6}$ 14. $\dfrac{5}{6} = \dfrac{20}{24}$ 15. $2 = \dfrac{8}{4}$

16. $\dfrac{1}{4} = \dfrac{4}{16}$ 17. $\dfrac{1}{8} = \dfrac{8}{64}$ 18. $\dfrac{2}{5} = \dfrac{12}{30}$

19. $\dfrac{2}{5} = \dfrac{4}{10}$ 20. $\dfrac{7}{8} = \dfrac{56}{64}$ 21. $\dfrac{2}{3} = \dfrac{10}{15}$

22. $\dfrac{3}{5} = \dfrac{9}{15}$ 23. $\dfrac{3}{4} = \dfrac{18}{24}$ 24. $\dfrac{7}{8} = \dfrac{49}{56}$

44   CD-104321 • © Carson-Dellosa

Adding Fractions with Like Denominators

Name _____ Date _____

Total Problems: **15**
Problems Correct: _____

Solve each problem. Write the answer in simplest form.

1. $\dfrac{1}{3} + \dfrac{2}{3} = $ **1**   2. $\dfrac{2}{9} + \dfrac{5}{9} = \dfrac{7}{9}$ 3. $\dfrac{1}{6} + \dfrac{1}{6} = \dfrac{1}{3}$

4. $\dfrac{3}{6} + \dfrac{1}{6} = \dfrac{2}{3}$ 5. $\dfrac{2}{4} + \dfrac{2}{4} = $ **1**   6. $\dfrac{1}{2} + \dfrac{1}{2} = $ **1**

7. $\dfrac{5}{8} + \dfrac{3}{8} = $ **1**   8. $\dfrac{5}{5} + \dfrac{2}{5} = 1\dfrac{2}{5}$ 9. $\dfrac{2}{10} + \dfrac{4}{10} = \dfrac{3}{5}$

10. $\dfrac{1}{2} + \dfrac{1}{2} = $ **1**   11. $\dfrac{3}{5} + \dfrac{2}{5} = $ **1**   12. $\dfrac{3}{7} + \dfrac{2}{7} = \dfrac{5}{7}$

13. $\dfrac{1}{3} + \dfrac{2}{3} = $ **1**   14. $\dfrac{1}{7} + \dfrac{1}{7} = \dfrac{2}{7}$ 15. $\dfrac{1}{6} + \dfrac{4}{6} = \dfrac{5}{6}$

CD-104321 • © Carson-Dellosa   45

Adding Fractions with Like Denominators

Name _____ Date _____

Total Problems: **20**
Problems Correct: _____

Solve each problem. Write the answer in simplest form.

1. $\dfrac{2}{7} + \dfrac{3}{7} = \dfrac{5}{7}$ 2. $\dfrac{6}{8} + \dfrac{1}{8} = \dfrac{7}{8}$ 3. $\dfrac{7}{10} + \dfrac{9}{10} = 1\dfrac{3}{5}$ 4. $\dfrac{3}{7} + \dfrac{1}{7} = \dfrac{4}{7}$ 5. $\dfrac{1}{5} + \dfrac{3}{5} = \dfrac{4}{5}$

6. $\dfrac{3}{5} + \dfrac{3}{5} = 1\dfrac{1}{5}$ 7. $\dfrac{1}{4} + \dfrac{2}{4} = \dfrac{3}{4}$ 8. $\dfrac{1}{5} + \dfrac{3}{5} = \dfrac{4}{5}$ 9. $\dfrac{4}{8} + \dfrac{2}{8} = \dfrac{3}{4}$ 10. $\dfrac{6}{7} + \dfrac{5}{7} = 1\dfrac{4}{7}$

11. $\dfrac{1}{8} + \dfrac{5}{8} = \dfrac{3}{4}$ 12. $\dfrac{2}{8} + \dfrac{4}{8} = \dfrac{3}{4}$ 13. $\dfrac{2}{10} + \dfrac{4}{10} = \dfrac{3}{5}$ 14. $\dfrac{3}{4} + \dfrac{2}{4} = 1\dfrac{1}{4}$ 15. $\dfrac{2}{3} + \dfrac{1}{3} = $ **1**

16. $\dfrac{4}{9} + \dfrac{3}{9} = \dfrac{7}{9}$ 17. $\dfrac{2}{6} + \dfrac{1}{6} = \dfrac{1}{2}$ 18. $\dfrac{5}{12} + \dfrac{5}{12} = \dfrac{5}{6}$ 19. $\dfrac{1}{6} + \dfrac{3}{6} = \dfrac{2}{3}$ 20. $\dfrac{2}{9} + \dfrac{1}{9} = \dfrac{1}{3}$

46   CD-104321 • © Carson-Dellosa

Adding Mixed Numbers with Like Denominators

Name _____ Date _____

Total Problems: **12**
Problems Correct: _____

Solve each problem. Write the answer in simplest form.

1. $2\dfrac{2}{5} + 2\dfrac{3}{5} = $ **5**   2. $5\dfrac{2}{7} + 6\dfrac{4}{7} = 11\dfrac{6}{7}$ 3. $3\dfrac{3}{8} + 4\dfrac{1}{8} = 7\dfrac{1}{2}$

4. $4\dfrac{2}{9} + 5\dfrac{3}{9} = 9\dfrac{5}{9}$ 5. $6\dfrac{5}{8} + 7\dfrac{2}{8} = 13\dfrac{7}{8}$ 6. $3\dfrac{3}{8} + 4\dfrac{1}{8} = 7\dfrac{1}{2}$

7. $8\dfrac{2}{5} + 1\dfrac{2}{5} = 9\dfrac{4}{5}$ 8. $7\dfrac{1}{8} + 7\dfrac{1}{8} = 14\dfrac{1}{4}$ 9. $2\dfrac{3}{4} + 2\dfrac{1}{4} = $ **5**

10. $5\dfrac{11}{15} + 6\dfrac{10}{15} = 12\dfrac{2}{5}$ 11. $2\dfrac{2}{5} + 2\dfrac{2}{5} = 4\dfrac{4}{5}$ 12. $4\dfrac{3}{4} + 1\dfrac{1}{4} = $ **6**

CD-104321 • © Carson-Dellosa   47

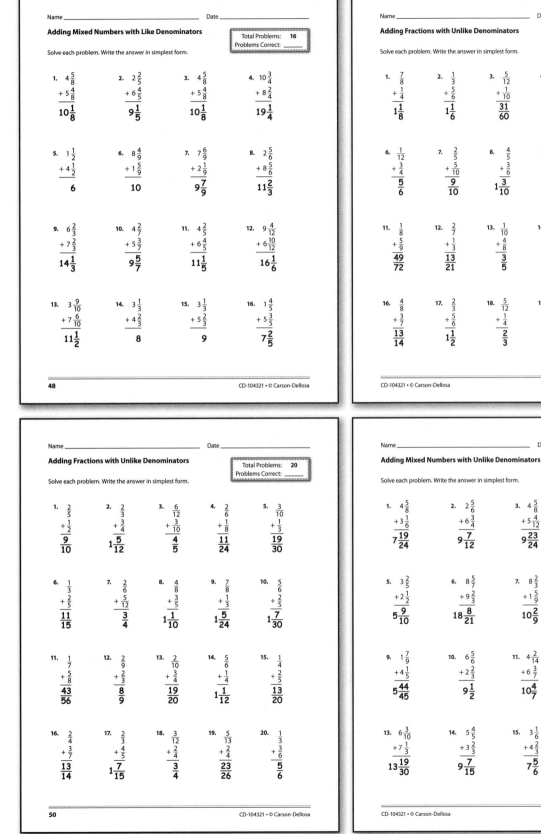

Worksheet (page 48)

Name _____ Date _____

Adding Mixed Numbers with Like Denominators

Total Problems: 16
Problems Correct: _____

Solve each problem. Write the answer in simplest form.

1. $4\frac{5}{8} + 5\frac{4}{8} = 10\frac{1}{8}$
2. $2\frac{2}{5} + 6\frac{4}{5} = 9\frac{1}{5}$
3. $4\frac{5}{8} + 5\frac{4}{8} = 10\frac{1}{8}$
4. $10\frac{3}{4} + 8\frac{2}{4} = 19\frac{1}{4}$

5. $1\frac{1}{2} + 4\frac{1}{2} = 6$
6. $8\frac{4}{9} + 1\frac{5}{9} = 10$
7. $7\frac{6}{9} + 2\frac{1}{9} = 9\frac{7}{9}$
8. $2\frac{5}{6} + 8\frac{5}{6} = 11\frac{2}{3}$

9. $6\frac{2}{3} + 7\frac{2}{3} = 14\frac{1}{3}$
10. $4\frac{2}{7} + 5\frac{3}{7} = 9\frac{5}{7}$
11. $4\frac{2}{5} + 6\frac{4}{5} = 11\frac{1}{5}$
12. $9\frac{4}{12} + 6\frac{10}{12} = 16\frac{1}{6}$

13. $3\frac{9}{10} + 7\frac{6}{10} = 11\frac{1}{2}$
14. $3\frac{1}{3} + 4\frac{2}{3} = 8$
15. $3\frac{1}{3} + 5\frac{2}{3} = 9$
16. $1\frac{4}{5} + 3\frac{3}{5} = 7\frac{2}{5}$

48   CD-104321 • © Carson-Dellosa

Worksheet (page 49)

Name _____ Date _____

Adding Fractions with Unlike Denominators

Total Problems: 20
Problems Correct: _____

Solve each problem. Write the answer in simplest form.

1. $\frac{7}{8} + \frac{1}{4} = 1\frac{1}{8}$
2. $\frac{1}{3} + \frac{5}{6} = 1\frac{1}{6}$
3. $\frac{5}{12} + \frac{1}{10} = \frac{31}{60}$
4. $\frac{2}{7} + \frac{1}{5} = \frac{17}{35}$
5. $\frac{3}{10} + \frac{4}{5} = 1\frac{1}{10}$

6. $\frac{1}{12} + \frac{3}{4} = \frac{5}{6}$
7. $\frac{2}{5} + \frac{5}{10} = \frac{9}{10}$
8. $\frac{4}{5} + \frac{3}{6} = 1\frac{3}{10}$
9. $\frac{1}{4} + \frac{1}{2} = \frac{3}{4}$
10. $\frac{2}{3} + \frac{4}{9} = 1\frac{1}{9}$

11. $\frac{1}{8} + \frac{5}{9} = \frac{49}{72}$
12. $\frac{2}{7} + \frac{1}{3} = \frac{13}{21}$
13. $\frac{1}{10} + \frac{4}{8} = \frac{3}{5}$
14. $\frac{5}{8} + \frac{1}{2} = 1\frac{1}{8}$
15. $\frac{2}{3} + \frac{1}{6} = \frac{5}{6}$

16. $\frac{4}{8} + \frac{3}{7} = \frac{13}{14}$
17. $\frac{2}{3} + \frac{5}{6} = 1\frac{1}{2}$
18. $\frac{5}{12} + \frac{1}{4} = \frac{2}{3}$
19. $\frac{6}{12} + \frac{7}{13} = 1\frac{1}{26}$
20. $\frac{1}{2} + \frac{3}{4} = 1\frac{1}{4}$

CD-104321 • © Carson-Dellosa   49

Worksheet (page 50)

Name _____ Date _____

Adding Fractions with Unlike Denominators

Total Problems: 20
Problems Correct: _____

Solve each problem. Write the answer in simplest form.

1. $\frac{2}{5} + \frac{1}{2} = \frac{9}{10}$
2. $\frac{2}{3} + \frac{3}{4} = 1\frac{5}{12}$
3. $\frac{6}{12} + \frac{3}{10} = \frac{4}{5}$
4. $\frac{2}{6} + \frac{1}{8} = \frac{11}{24}$
5. $\frac{3}{10} + \frac{1}{3} = \frac{19}{30}$

6. $\frac{1}{3} + \frac{2}{5} = \frac{11}{15}$
7. $\frac{2}{6} + \frac{5}{12} = \frac{3}{4}$
8. $\frac{4}{8} + \frac{3}{5} = 1\frac{1}{10}$
9. $\frac{7}{8} + \frac{1}{3} = 1\frac{5}{24}$
10. $\frac{5}{6} + \frac{2}{5} = 1\frac{7}{30}$

11. $\frac{1}{7} + \frac{5}{8} = \frac{43}{56}$
12. $\frac{2}{9} + \frac{2}{3} = \frac{8}{9}$
13. $\frac{2}{10} + \frac{3}{4} = \frac{19}{20}$
14. $\frac{5}{6} + \frac{1}{4} = 1\frac{1}{12}$
15. $\frac{1}{4} + \frac{2}{5} = \frac{13}{20}$

16. $\frac{2}{4} + \frac{3}{7} = \frac{13}{14}$
17. $\frac{2}{3} + \frac{4}{5} = 1\frac{7}{15}$
18. $\frac{3}{12} + \frac{2}{4} = \frac{3}{4}$
19. $\frac{5}{13} + \frac{2}{4} = \frac{23}{26}$
20. $\frac{1}{3} + \frac{3}{6} = \frac{5}{6}$

50   CD-104321 • © Carson-Dellosa

Worksheet (page 51)

Name _____ Date _____

Adding Mixed Numbers with Unlike Denominators

Total Problems: 16
Problems Correct: _____

Solve each problem. Write the answer in simplest form.

1. $4\frac{5}{8} + 3\frac{1}{6} = 7\frac{19}{24}$
2. $2\frac{5}{6} + 6\frac{3}{4} = 9\frac{7}{12}$
3. $4\frac{5}{8} + 5\frac{4}{12} = 9\frac{23}{24}$
4. $10\frac{3}{8} + 3\frac{1}{2} = 13\frac{7}{8}$

5. $3\frac{2}{5} + 2\frac{1}{2} = 5\frac{9}{10}$
6. $8\frac{5}{6} + 9\frac{2}{3} = 18\frac{8}{21}$
7. $8\frac{2}{3} + 1\frac{5}{9} = 10\frac{2}{9}$
8. $2\frac{3}{4} + 7\frac{1}{2} = 10\frac{1}{4}$

9. $1\frac{7}{9} + 4\frac{1}{5} = 5\frac{44}{45}$
10. $6\frac{5}{6} + 2\frac{2}{3} = 9\frac{1}{2}$
11. $4\frac{2}{14} + 6\frac{3}{7} = 10\frac{4}{7}$
12. $1\frac{1}{4} + 5\frac{10}{12} = 7\frac{1}{12}$

13. $6\frac{3}{10} + 7\frac{1}{3} = 13\frac{19}{30}$
14. $5\frac{4}{5} + 3\frac{2}{3} = 9\frac{7}{15}$
15. $3\frac{1}{6} + 4\frac{2}{3} = 7\frac{5}{6}$
16. $9\frac{1}{2} + 8\frac{3}{7} = 17\frac{13}{14}$

CD-104321 • © Carson-Dellosa   51

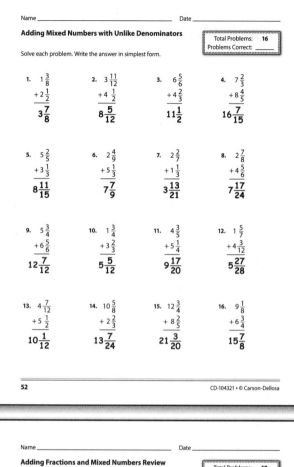

Worksheet 1 (page 52)

Name _____ Date _____

Adding Mixed Numbers with Unlike Denominators

Total Problems: **16**
Problems Correct: _____

Solve each problem. Write the answer in simplest form.

1. $1\frac{3}{8} + 2\frac{1}{2} = 3\frac{7}{8}$
2. $3\frac{11}{12} + 4\frac{1}{2} = 8\frac{5}{12}$
3. $6\frac{5}{6} + 4\frac{2}{3} = 11\frac{1}{2}$
4. $7\frac{2}{3} + 8\frac{4}{5} = 16\frac{7}{15}$

5. $5\frac{2}{5} + 3\frac{1}{3} = 8\frac{11}{15}$
6. $2\frac{4}{9} + 5\frac{1}{3} = 7\frac{7}{9}$
7. $2\frac{2}{7} + 1\frac{1}{3} = 3\frac{13}{21}$
8. $2\frac{7}{8} + 4\frac{5}{6} = 7\frac{17}{24}$

9. $5\frac{3}{4} + 6\frac{5}{6} = 12\frac{7}{12}$
10. $1\frac{3}{4} + 3\frac{2}{3} = 5\frac{5}{12}$
11. $4\frac{3}{5} + 5\frac{1}{4} = 9\frac{17}{20}$
12. $1\frac{5}{7} + 4\frac{3}{12} = 5\frac{27}{28}$

13. $4\frac{7}{12} + 5\frac{1}{2} = 10\frac{1}{12}$
14. $10\frac{5}{8} + 2\frac{2}{3} = 13\frac{7}{24}$
15. $12\frac{3}{4} + 8\frac{2}{5} = 21\frac{3}{20}$
16. $9\frac{1}{8} + 6\frac{3}{4} = 15\frac{7}{8}$

CD-104321 • © Carson-Dellosa

Worksheet 2 (page 53)

Name _____ Date _____

Adding Fractions and Mixed Numbers Review

Total Problems: **18**
Problems Correct: _____

Solve each problem. Write the answer in simplest form.

1. $2\frac{1}{3} + 4\frac{1}{3} = 6\frac{2}{3}$
2. $2\frac{3}{4} + 7\frac{1}{3} = 10\frac{1}{12}$
3. $\frac{1}{8} + \frac{1}{4} = \frac{3}{8}$

4. $\frac{3}{7} + \frac{1}{2} = \frac{13}{14}$
5. $\frac{2}{9} + \frac{2}{7} = \frac{32}{63}$
6. $6\frac{1}{9} + 3\frac{2}{9} = 9\frac{1}{3}$

7. $1\frac{3}{8} + 2\frac{1}{3} = 3\frac{17}{24}$
8. $\frac{2}{5} + \frac{1}{5} = \frac{3}{5}$
9. $\frac{4}{7} + \frac{1}{7} = \frac{5}{7}$

10. $\frac{5}{7} + \frac{2}{6} = 1\frac{1}{21}$
11. $1\frac{1}{6} + 2\frac{3}{8} = 3\frac{13}{24}$
12. $4\frac{10}{12} + 6\frac{11}{15} = 11\frac{17}{30}$

13. $\frac{3}{3} + \frac{1}{7} = 1\frac{1}{7}$
14. $\frac{3}{9} + \frac{2}{5} = \frac{11}{15}$
15. $\frac{4}{9} + \frac{9}{9} = 1\frac{4}{9}$

16. $\frac{1}{2} + \frac{2}{3} = 1\frac{1}{6}$
17. $\frac{4}{6} + \frac{2}{6} = 1$
18. $\frac{2}{3} + \frac{1}{5} = \frac{13}{15}$

CD-104321 • © Carson-Dellosa

Worksheet 3 (page 54)

Name _____ Date _____

Adding Fractions and Mixed Numbers Review

Total Problems: **18**
Problems Correct: _____

Solve each problem. Write the answer in simplest form.

1. $\frac{2}{3} + \frac{1}{5} = \frac{13}{15}$
2. $\frac{4}{5} + \frac{7}{8} = 1\frac{27}{40}$
3. $8\frac{1}{3} + 1\frac{1}{3} = 9\frac{2}{3}$
4. $11\frac{2}{3} + 9\frac{1}{5} = 20\frac{13}{15}$
5. $\frac{2}{10} + \frac{3}{5} = \frac{4}{5}$
6. $\frac{1}{10} + \frac{3}{5} = \frac{7}{10}$

7. $2\frac{4}{8} + 6\frac{5}{6} = 9\frac{1}{3}$
8. $3\frac{1}{6} + 2\frac{3}{6} = 5\frac{2}{3}$
9. $\frac{2}{7} + \frac{5}{7} = 1$
10. $\frac{4}{5} + \frac{1}{8} = \frac{37}{40}$
11. $\frac{3}{11} + \frac{4}{8} = \frac{17}{22}$
12. $\frac{2}{7} + \frac{1}{9} = \frac{25}{63}$

13. $4\frac{2}{7} + 6\frac{3}{7} = 10\frac{5}{7}$
14. $8\frac{3}{10} + 3\frac{10}{11} = 12\frac{23}{110}$
15. $\frac{3}{4} + \frac{1}{4} = 1$
16. $\frac{2}{12} + \frac{1}{8} = \frac{7}{24}$
17. $2\frac{1}{3} + 4\frac{2}{5} = 6\frac{11}{15}$
18. $1\frac{4}{6} + 5\frac{3}{6} = 7\frac{1}{6}$

CD-104321 • © Carson-Dellosa

Worksheet 4 (page 55)

Name _____ Date _____

Subtracting Fractions with Like Denominators

Total Problems: **20**
Problems Correct: _____

Solve each problem. Write the answer in simplest form.

1. $\frac{5}{6} - \frac{1}{6} = \frac{2}{3}$
2. $\frac{7}{12} - \frac{5}{12} = \frac{1}{6}$
3. $\frac{9}{14} - \frac{1}{14} = \frac{4}{7}$
4. $\frac{7}{8} - \frac{5}{8} = \frac{1}{4}$
5. $\frac{6}{8} - \frac{3}{8} = \frac{3}{8}$

6. $\frac{5}{7} - \frac{2}{7} = \frac{3}{7}$
7. $\frac{9}{11} - \frac{1}{11} = \frac{8}{11}$
8. $\frac{5}{9} - \frac{4}{9} = \frac{1}{9}$
9. $\frac{3}{10} - \frac{1}{10} = \frac{1}{5}$
10. $\frac{7}{9} - \frac{1}{9} = \frac{2}{3}$

11. $\frac{5}{8} - \frac{1}{8} = \frac{1}{2}$
12. $\frac{5}{7} - \frac{3}{7} = \frac{2}{7}$
13. $\frac{15}{16} - \frac{11}{16} = \frac{1}{4}$
14. $\frac{4}{5} - \frac{2}{5} = \frac{2}{5}$
15. $\frac{2}{3} - \frac{1}{3} = \frac{1}{3}$

16. $\frac{2}{5} - \frac{1}{5} = \frac{1}{5}$
17. $\frac{3}{4} - \frac{1}{4} = \frac{1}{2}$
18. $\frac{13}{15} - \frac{11}{15} = \frac{2}{15}$
19. $\frac{9}{10} - \frac{7}{10} = \frac{1}{5}$
20. $\frac{3}{3} - \frac{1}{3} = \frac{2}{3}$

CD-104321 • © Carson-Dellosa

Answer Key

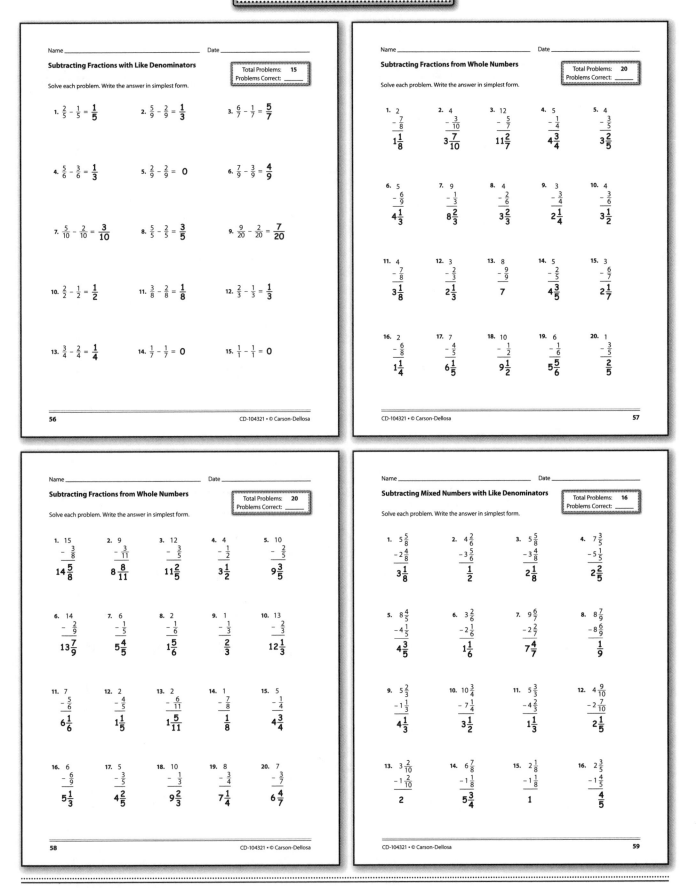

Subtracting Fractions with Like Denominators

Total Problems: 15
Problems Correct: _____

Solve each problem. Write the answer in simplest form.

1. $\frac{2}{5} - \frac{1}{5} = \frac{1}{5}$

2. $\frac{5}{9} - \frac{2}{9} = \frac{1}{3}$

3. $\frac{6}{7} - \frac{1}{7} = \frac{5}{7}$

4. $\frac{5}{6} - \frac{3}{6} = \frac{1}{3}$

5. $\frac{2}{9} - \frac{2}{9} = 0$

6. $\frac{7}{9} - \frac{3}{9} = \frac{4}{9}$

7. $\frac{5}{10} - \frac{2}{10} = \frac{3}{10}$

8. $\frac{5}{5} - \frac{2}{5} = \frac{3}{5}$

9. $\frac{9}{20} - \frac{2}{20} = \frac{7}{20}$

10. $\frac{2}{2} - \frac{1}{2} = \frac{1}{2}$

11. $\frac{3}{8} - \frac{2}{8} = \frac{1}{8}$

12. $\frac{2}{3} - \frac{1}{3} = \frac{1}{3}$

13. $\frac{3}{4} - \frac{2}{4} = \frac{1}{4}$

14. $\frac{1}{7} - \frac{1}{7} = 0$

15. $\frac{1}{1} - \frac{1}{1} = 0$

56   CD-104321 • © Carson-Dellosa

Subtracting Fractions from Whole Numbers

Total Problems: 20
Problems Correct: _____

Solve each problem. Write the answer in simplest form.

1. $2 - \frac{7}{8} = 1\frac{1}{8}$

2. $4 - \frac{3}{10} = 3\frac{7}{10}$

3. $12 - \frac{5}{7} = 11\frac{2}{7}$

4. $5 - \frac{1}{4} = 4\frac{3}{4}$

5. $4 - \frac{3}{5} = 3\frac{2}{5}$

6. $5 - \frac{6}{9} = 4\frac{1}{3}$

7. $9 - \frac{1}{3} = 8\frac{2}{3}$

8. $4 - \frac{2}{6} = 3\frac{2}{3}$

9. $3 - \frac{3}{4} = 2\frac{1}{4}$

10. $4 - \frac{3}{6} = 3\frac{1}{2}$

11. $4 - \frac{7}{8} = 3\frac{1}{8}$

12. $3 - \frac{2}{3} = 2\frac{1}{3}$

13. $8 - \frac{9}{9} = 7$

14. $5 - \frac{2}{5} = 4\frac{3}{5}$

15. $3 - \frac{6}{7} = 2\frac{1}{7}$

16. $2 - \frac{6}{8} = 1\frac{1}{4}$

17. $7 - \frac{4}{5} = 6\frac{1}{5}$

18. $10 - \frac{1}{2} = 9\frac{1}{2}$

19. $6 - \frac{1}{6} = 5\frac{5}{6}$

20. $1 - \frac{3}{5} = \frac{2}{5}$

CD-104321 • © Carson-Dellosa   57

Subtracting Fractions from Whole Numbers

Total Problems: 20
Problems Correct: _____

Solve each problem. Write the answer in simplest form.

1. $15 - \frac{3}{8} = 14\frac{5}{8}$

2. $9 - \frac{3}{11} = 8\frac{8}{11}$

3. $12 - \frac{3}{5} = 11\frac{2}{5}$

4. $4 - \frac{1}{2} = 3\frac{1}{2}$

5. $10 - \frac{2}{5} = 9\frac{3}{5}$

6. $14 - \frac{2}{9} = 13\frac{7}{9}$

7. $6 - \frac{1}{5} = 5\frac{4}{5}$

8. $2 - \frac{1}{6} = 1\frac{5}{6}$

9. $1 - \frac{1}{3} = \frac{2}{3}$

10. $13 - \frac{2}{3} = 12\frac{1}{3}$

11. $7 - \frac{5}{6} = 6\frac{1}{6}$

12. $2 - \frac{4}{5} = 1\frac{1}{5}$

13. $2 - \frac{6}{11} = 1\frac{5}{11}$

14. $1 - \frac{7}{8} = \frac{1}{8}$

15. $5 - \frac{1}{4} = 4\frac{3}{4}$

16. $6 - \frac{6}{9} = 5\frac{1}{3}$

17. $5 - \frac{3}{5} = 4\frac{2}{5}$

18. $10 - \frac{1}{3} = 9\frac{2}{3}$

19. $8 - \frac{3}{4} = 7\frac{1}{4}$

20. $7 - \frac{3}{7} = 6\frac{4}{7}$

58   CD-104321 • © Carson-Dellosa

Subtracting Mixed Numbers with Like Denominators

Total Problems: 16
Problems Correct: _____

Solve each problem. Write the answer in simplest form.

1. $5\frac{5}{8} - 2\frac{4}{8} = 3\frac{1}{8}$

2. $4\frac{2}{6} - 3\frac{5}{6} = \frac{1}{2}$

3. $5\frac{5}{8} - 3\frac{4}{8} = 2\frac{1}{8}$

4. $7\frac{3}{5} - 5\frac{1}{5} = 2\frac{2}{5}$

5. $8\frac{4}{5} - 4\frac{1}{5} = 4\frac{3}{5}$

6. $3\frac{2}{6} - 2\frac{1}{6} = 1\frac{1}{6}$

7. $9\frac{6}{7} - 2\frac{2}{7} = 7\frac{4}{7}$

8. $8\frac{7}{9} - 8\frac{6}{9} = \frac{1}{9}$

9. $5\frac{2}{3} - 1\frac{1}{3} = 4\frac{1}{3}$

10. $10\frac{3}{4} - 7\frac{1}{4} = 3\frac{1}{2}$

11. $5\frac{3}{3} - 4\frac{3}{3} = 1\frac{1}{3}$

12. $4\frac{9}{10} - 2\frac{7}{10} = 2\frac{1}{5}$

13. $3\frac{2}{10} - 1\frac{2}{10} = 2$

14. $6\frac{7}{8} - 1\frac{1}{8} = 5\frac{3}{4}$

15. $2\frac{1}{8} - 1\frac{8}{8} = 1$

16. $2\frac{3}{5} - 1\frac{4}{5} = \frac{4}{5}$

CD-104321 • © Carson-Dellosa   59

Worksheet 1 (page 60) — Subtracting Mixed Numbers with Like Denominators

Total Problems: 16
Problems Correct: _____

Solve each problem. Write the answer in simplest form.

1. $12\frac{7}{8} - 5\frac{5}{8} = 7\frac{1}{4}$
2. $2\frac{2}{3} - 2\frac{1}{3} = \frac{1}{3}$
3. $9\frac{7}{8} - 4\frac{4}{8} = 5\frac{3}{8}$
4. $3\frac{1}{8} - 1\frac{7}{8} = 1\frac{1}{4}$
5. $10\frac{2}{5} - 7\frac{4}{5} = 2\frac{3}{5}$
6. $3\frac{1}{4} - 2\frac{3}{4} = \frac{1}{2}$
7. $10\frac{2}{3} - 9\frac{1}{3} = 1\frac{1}{3}$
8. $5\frac{4}{5} - 4\frac{1}{5} = 1\frac{3}{5}$
9. $5\frac{2}{3} - 1\frac{1}{3} = 4\frac{1}{3}$
10. $8\frac{7}{10} - 7\frac{9}{10} = \frac{4}{5}$
11. $8\frac{3}{16} - 7\frac{5}{16} = \frac{7}{8}$
12. $6\frac{7}{15} - 2\frac{8}{15} = 3\frac{14}{15}$
13. $6\frac{2}{12} - 3\frac{2}{12} = 3$
14. $4\frac{5}{6} - 2\frac{1}{6} = 2\frac{2}{3}$
15. $4\frac{11}{18} - 1\frac{7}{18} = 3\frac{2}{9}$
16. $8\frac{7}{10} - 1\frac{3}{10} = 7\frac{2}{5}$

Worksheet 2 (page 61) — Subtracting Fractions with Unlike Denominators

Total Problems: 20
Problems Correct: _____

Solve each problem. Write the answer in simplest form.

1. $\frac{1}{3} - \frac{1}{4} = \frac{1}{12}$
2. $\frac{3}{4} - \frac{1}{5} = \frac{11}{20}$
3. $\frac{9}{10} - \frac{5}{7} = \frac{13}{70}$
4. $\frac{5}{7} - \frac{2}{9} = \frac{31}{63}$
5. $\frac{3}{5} - \frac{1}{3} = \frac{4}{15}$
6. $\frac{3}{8} - \frac{2}{6} = \frac{1}{24}$
7. $\frac{2}{4} - \frac{1}{3} = \frac{1}{6}$
8. $\frac{1}{5} - \frac{1}{8} = \frac{3}{40}$
9. $\frac{7}{12} - \frac{1}{4} = \frac{1}{3}$
10. $\frac{3}{9} - \frac{1}{4} = \frac{1}{12}$
11. $\frac{7}{8} - \frac{1}{9} = \frac{55}{72}$
12. $\frac{8}{8} - \frac{4}{6} = \frac{1}{3}$
13. $\frac{2}{3} - \frac{1}{2} = \frac{1}{6}$
14. $\frac{2}{3} - \frac{4}{9} = \frac{2}{9}$
15. $\frac{1}{3} - \frac{1}{6} = \frac{1}{6}$
16. $\frac{8}{9} - \frac{3}{6} = \frac{7}{18}$
17. $\frac{5}{6} - \frac{1}{5} = \frac{19}{30}$
18. $\frac{7}{8} - \frac{3}{10} = \frac{23}{40}$
19. $\frac{9}{12} - \frac{2}{11} = \frac{25}{44}$
20. $\frac{6}{6} - \frac{3}{12} = \frac{3}{4}$

Worksheet 3 (page 62) — Subtracting Fractions with Unlike Denominators

Total Problems: 20
Problems Correct: _____

Solve each problem. Write the answer in simplest form.

1. $\frac{3}{4} - \frac{1}{6} = \frac{7}{12}$
2. $\frac{13}{15} - \frac{2}{3} = \frac{1}{5}$
3. $\frac{2}{3} - \frac{7}{12} = \frac{1}{12}$
4. $\frac{5}{6} - \frac{1}{3} = \frac{1}{2}$
5. $\frac{5}{6} - \frac{2}{5} = \frac{13}{30}$
6. $\frac{2}{3} - \frac{1}{6} = \frac{1}{2}$
7. $\frac{11}{14} - \frac{1}{2} = \frac{2}{7}$
8. $\frac{7}{12} - \frac{1}{4} = \frac{1}{3}$
9. $\frac{11}{12} - \frac{1}{6} = \frac{3}{4}$
10. $\frac{5}{6} - \frac{3}{7} = \frac{17}{42}$
11. $\frac{7}{8} - \frac{1}{9} = \frac{55}{72}$
12. $\frac{5}{6} - \frac{1}{2} = \frac{1}{3}$
13. $\frac{5}{12} - \frac{1}{3} = \frac{1}{12}$
14. $\frac{7}{8} - \frac{1}{6} = \frac{17}{24}$
15. $\frac{1}{3} - \frac{1}{6} = \frac{1}{6}$
16. $\frac{2}{3} - \frac{4}{9} = \frac{2}{9}$
17. $\frac{3}{4} - \frac{1}{3} = \frac{5}{12}$
18. $\frac{8}{9} - \frac{5}{6} = \frac{1}{18}$
19. $\frac{9}{12} - \frac{2}{11} = \frac{25}{44}$
20. $\frac{5}{6} - \frac{1}{8} = \frac{17}{24}$

Worksheet 4 (page 63) — Subtracting Mixed Numbers with Unlike Denominators

Total Problems: 16
Problems Correct: _____

Solve each problem. Write the answer in simplest form.

1. $2\frac{2}{3} - 1\frac{1}{2} = 1\frac{1}{6}$
2. $4\frac{1}{3} - 2\frac{3}{8} = 1\frac{23}{24}$
3. $3\frac{5}{6} - 2\frac{1}{12} = 1\frac{3}{4}$
4. $5\frac{5}{8} - 2\frac{3}{4} = 2\frac{7}{8}$
5. $4\frac{7}{10} - 1\frac{2}{5} = 3\frac{3}{10}$
6. $3\frac{7}{8} - 2\frac{1}{6} = 1\frac{17}{24}$
7. $5\frac{4}{9} - 2\frac{1}{3} = 3\frac{1}{9}$
8. $3\frac{1}{2} - 1\frac{3}{4} = 1\frac{3}{4}$
9. $4\frac{1}{3} - 1\frac{2}{5} = 2\frac{14}{15}$
10. $5\frac{5}{12} - 3\frac{7}{10} = 1\frac{43}{60}$
11. $3\frac{5}{6} - 1\frac{5}{9} = 2\frac{5}{18}$
12. $7\frac{3}{5} - 4\frac{7}{10} = 2\frac{9}{10}$
13. $6\frac{2}{4} - 4\frac{1}{2} = 2$
14. $4\frac{7}{8} - 2\frac{1}{4} = 2\frac{5}{8}$
15. $4\frac{2}{5} - 2\frac{3}{10} = 2\frac{1}{10}$
16. $6\frac{4}{5} - 5\frac{3}{7} = 1\frac{13}{35}$

Page 64

Name _____ Date _____

Subtracting Mixed Numbers with Unlike Denominators

Total Problems: **16**
Problems Correct: _____

Solve each problem. Write the answer in simplest form.

1. $5\frac{1}{6}$
$-2\frac{3}{4}$
$2\frac{5}{12}$

2. $4\frac{7}{10}$
$-1\frac{4}{5}$
$2\frac{9}{10}$

3. $5\frac{7}{8}$
$-1\frac{1}{16}$
$4\frac{13}{16}$

4. $3\frac{1}{3}$
$-1\frac{5}{6}$
$1\frac{1}{2}$

5. $4\frac{1}{3}$
$-1\frac{1}{4}$
$3\frac{1}{12}$

6. $3\frac{7}{12}$
$-1\frac{9}{10}$
$1\frac{41}{60}$

7. $5\frac{4}{5}$
$-1\frac{9}{10}$
$3\frac{9}{10}$

8. $4\frac{3}{4}$
$-1\frac{5}{6}$
$2\frac{11}{12}$

9. $6\frac{1}{2}$
$-\frac{1}{3}$
$6\frac{1}{6}$

10. $7\frac{1}{4}$
$-3\frac{2}{3}$
$3\frac{7}{12}$

11. $10\frac{4}{5}$
$-6\frac{5}{6}$
$3\frac{29}{30}$

12. $12\frac{2}{3}$
$-9\frac{6}{7}$
$2\frac{17}{21}$

13. $5\frac{1}{3}$
$-3\frac{3}{4}$
$1\frac{7}{12}$

14. $8\frac{2}{5}$
$-4\frac{1}{4}$
$4\frac{3}{20}$

15. $2\frac{2}{3}$
$-2\frac{1}{4}$
$\frac{5}{12}$

16. $6\frac{1}{3}$
$-5\frac{3}{4}$
$\frac{7}{12}$

CD-104321 • © Carson-Dellosa

Page 65

Name _____ Date _____

Multiplying Fractions

Total Problems: **15**
Problems Correct: _____

Solve each problem. Write the answer in simplest form.

1. $\frac{3}{4} \times \frac{2}{5} = \frac{3}{10}$

2. $\frac{7}{8} \times \frac{1}{6} = \frac{7}{48}$

3. $\frac{4}{5} \times \frac{2}{3} = \frac{8}{15}$

4. $\frac{1}{3} \times \frac{1}{5} = \frac{1}{15}$

5. $\frac{2}{7} \times \frac{2}{9} = \frac{4}{63}$

6. $\frac{1}{4} \times \frac{3}{5} = \frac{3}{20}$

7. $\frac{4}{7} \times \frac{3}{8} = \frac{3}{14}$

8. $\frac{2}{3} \times \frac{2}{5} = \frac{4}{15}$

9. $\frac{2}{3} \times \frac{4}{5} = \frac{8}{15}$

10. $\frac{3}{5} \times \frac{1}{3} = \frac{1}{5}$

11. $\frac{1}{8} \times \frac{2}{5} = \frac{1}{20}$

12. $\frac{1}{6} \times \frac{2}{3} = \frac{1}{9}$

13. $\frac{1}{2} \times \frac{3}{4} = \frac{3}{8}$

14. $\frac{1}{8} \times \frac{1}{3} = \frac{1}{24}$

15. $\frac{1}{6} \times \frac{4}{5} = \frac{2}{15}$

CD-104321 • © Carson-Dellosa

Page 66

Name _____ Date _____

Multiplying Fractions

Total Problems: **15**
Problems Correct: _____

Solve each problem. Write the answer in simplest form.

1. $\frac{1}{3} \times \frac{1}{7} = \frac{1}{21}$

2. $\frac{3}{5} \times \frac{2}{9} = \frac{2}{15}$

3. $\frac{1}{6} \times \frac{4}{5} = \frac{2}{15}$

4. $\frac{2}{7} \times \frac{5}{8} = \frac{5}{28}$

5. $\frac{2}{5} \times \frac{4}{9} = \frac{8}{45}$

6. $\frac{1}{4} \times \frac{1}{6} = \frac{1}{24}$

7. $\frac{2}{3} \times \frac{3}{8} = \frac{1}{4}$

8. $\frac{3}{4} \times \frac{4}{7} = \frac{3}{7}$

9. $\frac{2}{5} \times \frac{5}{6} = \frac{1}{3}$

10. $\frac{4}{5} \times \frac{2}{3} = \frac{8}{15}$

11. $\frac{1}{5} \times \frac{5}{6} = \frac{1}{6}$

12. $\frac{1}{2} \times \frac{3}{7} = \frac{3}{14}$

13. $\frac{2}{5} \times \frac{4}{9} = \frac{8}{45}$

14. $\frac{2}{8} \times \frac{3}{3} = \frac{1}{4}$

15. $\frac{1}{7} \times \frac{6}{8} = \frac{3}{28}$

CD-104321 • © Carson-Dellosa

Page 67

Name _____ Date _____

Multiplying Fractions and Whole Numbers

Total Problems: **15**
Problems Correct: _____

Solve each problem. Write the answer in simplest form.

1. $4 \times \frac{1}{2} = 2$

2. $2 \times \frac{2}{5} = \frac{4}{5}$

3. $4 \times \frac{2}{7} = 1\frac{1}{7}$

4. $3 \times \frac{5}{6} = 2\frac{1}{2}$

5. $8 \times \frac{1}{8} = 1$

6. $\frac{2}{5} \times 3 = 1\frac{1}{5}$

7. $\frac{1}{8} \times 5 = \frac{5}{8}$

8. $\frac{5}{7} \times 5 = 3\frac{4}{7}$

9. $\frac{2}{3} \times 2 = 1\frac{1}{3}$

10. $\frac{3}{9} \times 4 = 1\frac{1}{3}$

11. $\frac{1}{3} \times 7 = 2\frac{1}{3}$

12. $4 \times \frac{3}{4} = 3$

13. $\frac{6}{8} \times 2 = 1\frac{1}{2}$

14. $5 \times \frac{4}{5} = 4$

15. $3 \times \frac{2}{3} = 2$

CD-104321 • © Carson-Dellosa

Answer Key

Multiplying Fractions and Whole Numbers (p. 68)

Name _____ Date _____

Solve each problem. Write the answer in simplest form.

Total Problems: 15
Problems Correct: _____

1. $5 \times \frac{2}{5} =$ **2**
2. $8 \times \frac{1}{7} =$ **$1\frac{1}{7}$**
3. $6 \times \frac{3}{8} =$ **$2\frac{1}{4}$**

4. $4 \times \frac{8}{9} =$ **$3\frac{5}{9}$**
5. $2 \times \frac{3}{7} =$ **$\frac{6}{7}$**
6. $\frac{2}{3} \times 4 =$ **$2\frac{2}{3}$**

7. $\frac{1}{9} \times 6 =$ **$\frac{2}{3}$**
8. $\frac{5}{6} \times 4 =$ **$3\frac{1}{3}$**
9. $\frac{4}{6} \times 3 =$ **2**

10. $\frac{4}{5} \times 6 =$ **$4\frac{4}{5}$**
11. $\frac{3}{4} \times 5 =$ **$3\frac{3}{4}$**
12. $2 \times \frac{4}{5} =$ **$1\frac{3}{5}$**

13. $\frac{2}{7} \times 6 =$ **$1\frac{5}{7}$**
14. $7 \times \frac{3}{5} =$ **$4\frac{1}{5}$**
15. $7 \times \frac{5}{6} =$ **$5\frac{5}{6}$**

68 CD-104321 • © Carson-Dellosa

Multiplying Fractions and Whole Numbers (p. 69)

Name _____ Date _____

Solve each problem. Write the answer in simplest form.

Total Problems: 15
Problems Correct: _____

1. $10 \times \frac{2}{3} =$ **$6\frac{2}{3}$**
2. $4 \times \frac{4}{7} =$ **$2\frac{2}{7}$**
3. $7 \times \frac{10}{11} =$ **$6\frac{4}{11}$**

4. $36 \times \frac{2}{288} =$ **$\frac{1}{4}$**
5. $6 \times \frac{4}{8} =$ **3**
6. $9 \times \frac{5}{6} =$ **$7\frac{1}{2}$**

7. $3 \times \frac{1}{3} =$ **1**
8. $30 \times \frac{3}{90} =$ **1**
9. $12 \times \frac{1}{36} =$ **$\frac{1}{3}$**

10. $5 \times \frac{2}{5} =$ **2**
11. $12 \times \frac{7}{8} =$ **$10\frac{1}{2}$**
12. $5 \times \frac{3}{4} =$ **$3\frac{3}{4}$**

13. $22 \times \frac{1}{44} =$ **$\frac{1}{2}$**
14. $4 \times \frac{1}{8} =$ **$\frac{1}{2}$**
15. $8 \times \frac{2}{3} =$ **$5\frac{1}{3}$**

CD-104321 • © Carson-Dellosa 69

Multiplying Mixed Numbers and Whole Numbers (p. 70)

Name _____ Date _____

Solve each problem. Write the answer in simplest form.

Total Problems: 12
Problems Correct: _____

1. $2 \times 2\frac{1}{3} =$ **$4\frac{2}{3}$**
2. $3 \times 5\frac{1}{5} =$ **$15\frac{3}{5}$**
3. $9 \times 3\frac{2}{3} =$ **33**

4. $8 \times 9\frac{1}{10} =$ **$72\frac{4}{5}$**
5. $4 \times 5\frac{1}{8} =$ **$20\frac{1}{2}$**
6. $6 \times 3\frac{1}{6} =$ **19**

7. $5 \times 6\frac{5}{8} =$ **$33\frac{1}{8}$**
8. $3 \times 9\frac{1}{3} =$ **28**
9. $7 \times 1\frac{3}{4} =$ **$12\frac{1}{4}$**

10. $7 \times 2\frac{3}{5} =$ **$18\frac{1}{5}$**
11. $4 \times 2\frac{1}{2} =$ **10**
12. $7 \times 2\frac{1}{7} =$ **15**

70 CD-104321 • © Carson-Dellosa

Multiplying Mixed Numbers and Whole Numbers (p. 71)

Name _____ Date _____

Solve each problem. Write the answer in simplest form.

Total Problems: 12
Problems Correct: _____

1. $4 \times 3\frac{3}{5} =$ **$14\frac{2}{5}$**
2. $6 \times 9\frac{4}{5} =$ **$58\frac{4}{5}$**
3. $2 \times 8\frac{3}{4} =$ **$17\frac{1}{2}$**

4. $9 \times 1\frac{1}{18} =$ **$9\frac{1}{2}$**
5. $10 \times 5\frac{1}{2} =$ **55**
6. $8 \times 2\frac{3}{8} =$ **19**

7. $5 \times 4\frac{2}{5} =$ **22**
8. $2 \times 7\frac{5}{8} =$ **$15\frac{1}{4}$**
9. $2 \times 5\frac{1}{8} =$ **$10\frac{1}{4}$**

10. $3 \times 1\frac{15}{16} =$ **$5\frac{13}{16}$**
11. $4 \times 8\frac{6}{7} =$ **$35\frac{3}{7}$**
12. $2 \times 2\frac{1}{4} =$ **$4\frac{1}{2}$**

CD-104321 • © Carson-Dellosa 71

Page 72

Name _____ Date _____

Multiplying Mixed Numbers

| Total Problems: | 12 |
| Problems Correct: | ___ |

Solve each problem. Write the answer in simplest form.

1. $3\frac{1}{2} \times 2\frac{1}{2} = 8\frac{3}{4}$ 2. $8\frac{5}{6} \times 3\frac{6}{7} = 34\frac{1}{14}$ 3. $4\frac{2}{5} \times 6\frac{2}{3} = 29\frac{1}{3}$

4. $4\frac{2}{9} \times 5\frac{10}{11} = 24\frac{94}{99}$ 5. $2\frac{2}{3} \times 4\frac{2}{5} = 11\frac{11}{15}$ 6. $5\frac{3}{4} \times 6\frac{1}{4} = 35\frac{15}{16}$

7. $2\frac{8}{9} \times 7\frac{7}{8} = 22\frac{3}{4}$ 8. $7\frac{1}{4} \times 3\frac{3}{7} = 24\frac{6}{7}$ 9. $6\frac{7}{8} \times 3\frac{1}{3} = 22\frac{11}{12}$

10. $7\frac{9}{10} \times 8\frac{7}{8} = 70\frac{9}{80}$ 11. $4\frac{1}{4} \times 3\frac{5}{6} = 16\frac{7}{24}$ 12. $8\frac{3}{5} \times 1\frac{1}{2} = 12\frac{9}{10}$

72   CD-104321 • © Carson-Dellosa

Page 73

Name _____ Date _____

Multiplying Mixed Numbers

| Total Problems: | 8 |
| Problems Correct: | ___ |

Solve each problem. Write the answer in simplest form.

1. $8\frac{1}{4} \times 6\frac{2}{3} = 55$ 2. $7\frac{2}{5} \times 6\frac{2}{3} = 49\frac{1}{3}$

3. $2\frac{5}{6} \times 12\frac{4}{5} = 36\frac{4}{15}$ 4. $4\frac{2}{7} \times 6\frac{1}{10} = 26\frac{1}{7}$

5. $5\frac{1}{5} \times 4\frac{1}{3} = 22\frac{8}{15}$ 6. $9\frac{9}{10} \times 4\frac{7}{8} = 48\frac{21}{80}$

7. $1\frac{10}{13} \times 2\frac{9}{13} = 4\frac{129}{169}$ 8. $8\frac{3}{5} \times 4\frac{5}{6} = 41\frac{17}{30}$

CD-104321 • © Carson-Dellosa   73

Page 74

Name _____ Date _____

Adding Decimals

| Total Problems: | 23 |
| Problems Correct: | ___ |

Solve each problem. Regroup when necessary.

| 1. 14.2 $+12.1$ $\overline{26.3}$ | 2. 18.7 $+10.5$ $\overline{29.2}$ | 3. 1.47 $+6.54$ $\overline{8.01}$ | 4. 12.3 $+15.2$ $\overline{27.5}$ | 5. 16.6 $+13.8$ $\overline{30.4}$ | 6. 7.85 $+9.41$ $\overline{17.26}$ |

| 7. 18.2 $+16.5$ $\overline{34.7}$ | 8. 15.2 $+13.0$ $\overline{28.2}$ | 9. 2.22 $+3.94$ $\overline{6.16}$ | 10. 22.2 $+13.1$ $\overline{35.3}$ | 11. 12.0 $+14.9$ $\overline{26.9}$ | 12. 7.54 $+2.24$ $\overline{9.78}$ |

| 13. 47.5 $+32.6$ $\overline{80.1}$ | 14. 49.4 $+11.1$ $\overline{60.5}$ | 15. 8.85 $+7.33$ $\overline{16.18}$ | 16. 54.8 $+13.2$ $\overline{68.0}$ | 17. 4.58 $+2.31$ $\overline{6.89}$ |

18. $12.95 + 5.06 = 18.01$ 19. $13.8 + 6.9 = 20.7$

20. $46.02 + 75.67 = 121.69$ 21. $16.3 + 35.7 = 52.0$

22. $3.25 + 3.25 = 6.50$ 23. $87.01 + 16.53 = 103.54$

74   CD-104321 • © Carson-Dellosa

Page 75

Name _____ Date _____

Adding Decimals

| Total Problems: | 14 |
| Problems Correct: | ___ |

Solve each problem. Regroup when necessary.

| 1. 4.15 6.20 $+8.63$ $\overline{18.98}$ | 2. 8.461 0.003 $+0.212$ $\overline{8.676}$ | 3. 33.421 7.35 $+42.6$ $\overline{83.371}$ | 4. 2.26 3.43 $+8.15$ $\overline{13.84}$ |

| 5. 0.491 0.320 $+0.617$ $\overline{1.428}$ | 6. 22.444 1.908 $+0.076$ $\overline{24.428}$ | 7. 32.15 64.23 $+32.57$ $\overline{128.95}$ | 8. 14.501 62.037 $+8.693$ $\overline{85.231}$ |

| 9. 62.561 0.179 $+2.602$ $\overline{65.342}$ | 10. 3.564 1.508 $+1.521$ $\overline{6.593}$ | 11. 62.715 1.307 $+0.032$ $\overline{64.054}$ | 12. 16.201 7.35 $+2.9$ $\overline{26.451}$ |

13. $8.16 + 15.204 + 35.8 = 59.164$ 14. $0.007 + 1.12 + 5.978 = 7.105$

CD-104321 • © Carson-Dellosa   75

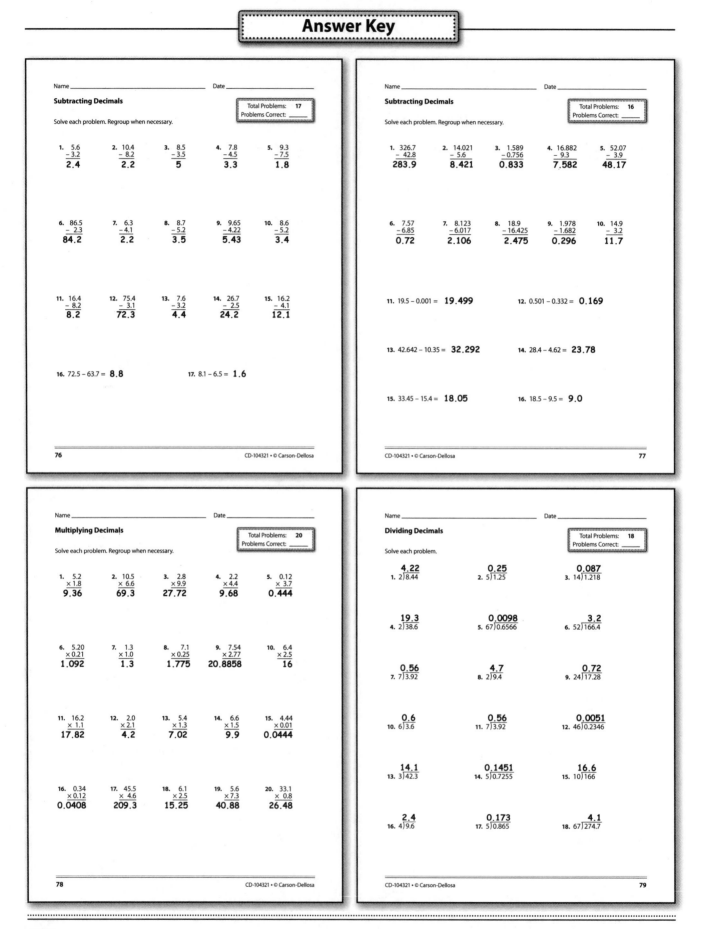

Name _____ Date _____

Subtracting Decimals

Total Problems:	17
Problems Correct:	_____

Solve each problem. Regroup when necessary.

1. 5.6
    − 3.2
    2.4

2. 10.4
    − 8.2
    2.2

3. 8.5
    − 3.5
    5

4. 7.8
    − 4.5
    3.3

5. 9.3
    − 7.5
    1.8

6. 86.5
    − 2.3
    84.2

7. 6.3
    − 4.1
    2.2

8. 8.7
    − 5.2
    3.5

9. 9.65
    − 4.22
    5.43

10. 8.6
    − 5.2
    3.4

11. 16.4
    − 8.2
    8.2

12. 75.4
    − 3.1
    72.3

13. 7.6
    − 3.2
    4.4

14. 26.7
    − 2.5
    24.2

15. 16.2
    − 4.1
    12.1

16. 72.5 − 63.7 = **8.8**

17. 8.1 − 6.5 = **1.6**

76   CD-104321 • © Carson-Dellosa

Name _____ Date _____

Subtracting Decimals

Total Problems:	16
Problems Correct:	_____

Solve each problem. Regroup when necessary.

1. 326.7
    − 42.8
    283.9

2. 14.021
    − 5.6
    8.421

3. 1.589
    − 0.756
    0.833

4. 16.882
    − 9.3
    7.582

5. 52.07
    − 3.9
    48.17

6. 7.57
    − 6.85
    0.72

7. 8.123
    − 6.017
    2.106

8. 18.9
    − 16.425
    2.475

9. 1.978
    − 1.682
    0.296

10. 14.9
    − 3.2
    11.7

11. 19.5 − 0.001 = **19.499**

12. 0.501 − 0.332 = **0.169**

13. 42.642 − 10.35 = **32.292**

14. 28.4 − 4.62 = **23.78**

15. 33.45 − 15.4 = **18.05**

16. 18.5 − 9.5 = **9.0**

CD-104321 • © Carson-Dellosa   77

Name _____ Date _____

Multiplying Decimals

Total Problems:	20
Problems Correct:	_____

Solve each problem. Regroup when necessary.

1. 5.2
    × 1.8
    9.36

2. 10.5
    × 6.6
    69.3

3. 2.8
    × 9.9
    27.72

4. 2.2
    × 4.4
    9.68

5. 0.12
    × 3.7
    0.444

6. 5.20
    × 0.21
    1.092

7. 1.3
    × 1.0
    1.3

8. 7.1
    × 0.25
    1.775

9. 7.54
    × 2.77
    20.8858

10. 6.4
    × 2.5
    16

11. 16.2
    × 1.1
    17.82

12. 2.0
    × 2.1
    4.2

13. 5.4
    × 1.3
    7.02

14. 6.6
    × 1.5
    9.9

15. 4.44
    × 0.01
    0.0444

16. 0.34
    × 0.12
    0.0408

17. 45.5
    × 4.6
    209.3

18. 6.1
    × 2.5
    15.25

19. 5.6
    × 7.3
    40.88

20. 33.1
    × 0.8
    26.48

78   CD-104321 • © Carson-Dellosa

Name _____ Date _____

Dividing Decimals

Total Problems:	18
Problems Correct:	_____

Solve each problem.

1. **4.22**
    2)8.44

2. **0.25**
    5)1.25

3. **0.087**
    14)1.218

4. **19.3**
    2)38.6

5. **0.0098**
    67)0.6566

6. **3.2**
    52)166.4

7. **0.56**
    7)3.92

8. **4.7**
    2)9.4

9. **0.72**
    24)17.28

10. **0.6**
    6)3.6

11. **0.56**
    7)3.92

12. **0.0051**
    46)0.2346

13. **14.1**
    3)42.3

14. **0.1451**
    5)0.7255

15. **16.6**
    10)166

16. **2.4**
    4)9.6

17. **0.173**
    5)0.865

18. **4.1**
    67)274.7

CD-104321 • © Carson-Dellosa   79

Name _____ Date _____

Dividing Decimals

Total Problems: **18**
Problems Correct: _____

Solve each problem.

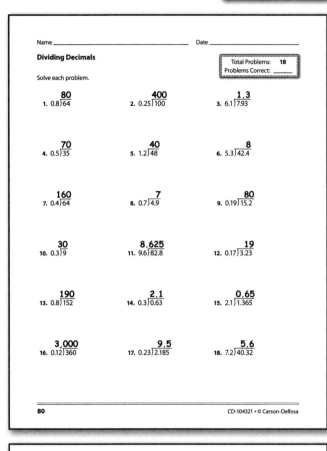

1. $0.8\overline{)64}$ → **80**

2. $0.25\overline{)100}$ → **400**

3. $6.1\overline{)7.93}$ → **1.3**

4. $0.5\overline{)35}$ → **70**

5. $1.2\overline{)48}$ → **40**

6. $5.3\overline{)42.4}$ → **8**

7. $0.4\overline{)64}$ → **160**

8. $0.7\overline{)4.9}$ → **7**

9. $0.19\overline{)15.2}$ → **80**

10. $0.3\overline{)9}$ → **30**

11. $9.6\overline{)82.8}$ → **8.625**

12. $0.17\overline{)3.23}$ → **19**

13. $0.8\overline{)152}$ → **190**

14. $0.3\overline{)0.63}$ → **2.1**

15. $2.1\overline{)1.365}$ → **0.65**

16. $0.12\overline{)360}$ → **3,000**

17. $0.23\overline{)2.185}$ → **9.5**

18. $7.2\overline{)40.32}$ → **5.6**

80

CD-104321 • © Carson-Dellosa

Name _____ Date _____

Writing Decimals as Fractions

Total Problems: **24**
Problems Correct: _____

Write each decimal as a fraction in simplest form.

1. $0.5 = \frac{1}{2}$

2. $0.9 = \frac{9}{10}$

3. $0.7 = \frac{7}{10}$

4. $9.5 = 9\frac{1}{2}$

5. $1.8 = 1\frac{4}{5}$

6. $2.2 = 2\frac{1}{5}$

7. $6.2 = 6\frac{1}{5}$

8. $1.25 = 1\frac{1}{4}$

9. $0.1 = \frac{1}{10}$

10. $0.22 = \frac{11}{50}$

11. $4.1 = 4\frac{1}{10}$

12. $3.6 = 3\frac{3}{5}$

13. $7.3 = 7\frac{3}{10}$

14. $3.9 = 3\frac{9}{10}$

15. $8.8 = 8\frac{4}{5}$

16. $2.5 = 2\frac{1}{2}$

17. $0.4 = \frac{2}{5}$

18. $0.8 = \frac{4}{5}$

19. $5.2 = 5\frac{1}{5}$

20. $2.5 = 2\frac{1}{2}$

21. $6.5 = 6\frac{1}{2}$

22. $4.2 = 4\frac{1}{5}$

23. $4.1 = 4\frac{1}{10}$

24. $9.3 = 9\frac{3}{10}$

CD-104321 • © Carson-Dellosa

81

Name _____ Date _____

Writing Decimals as Fractions

Total Problems: **24**
Problems Correct: _____

Write each decimal as a fraction in simplest form.

1. $8.2 = 8\frac{1}{5}$

2. $5.4 = 5\frac{2}{5}$

3. $48.2 = 48\frac{1}{5}$

4. $0.15 = \frac{3}{20}$

5. $25.32 = 25\frac{8}{25}$

6. $3.25 = 3\frac{1}{4}$

7. $30.2 = 30\frac{1}{5}$

8. $0.625 = \frac{5}{8}$

9. $9.1 = 9\frac{1}{10}$

10. $10.6 = 10\frac{3}{5}$

11. $0.25 = \frac{1}{4}$

12. $0.68 = \frac{17}{25}$

13. $86.12 = 86\frac{3}{25}$

14. $6.5 = 6\frac{1}{2}$

15. $9.12 = 9\frac{3}{25}$

16. $0.125 = \frac{1}{8}$

17. $7.6 = 7\frac{3}{5}$

18. $25.3 = 25\frac{3}{10}$

19. $0.75 = \frac{3}{4}$

20. $4.36 = 4\frac{9}{25}$

21. $9.45 = 9\frac{9}{20}$

22. $75.2 = 75\frac{1}{5}$

23. $25.2 = 25\frac{1}{5}$

24. $25.6 = 25\frac{3}{5}$

82

CD-104321 • © Carson-Dellosa

Name _____ Date _____

Writing Fractions as Decimals

Total Problems: **18**
Problems Correct: _____

Write each fraction as a decimal. Round to the nearest thousandth when necessary.

1. $\frac{5}{8} = 0.625$

2. $\frac{1}{8} = 0.125$

3. $\frac{1}{5} = 0.2$

4. $\frac{1}{12} = 0.083$

5. $\frac{1}{20} = 0.05$

6. $\frac{5}{9} = 0.556$

7. $\frac{1}{4} = 0.25$

8. $\frac{7}{8} = 0.875$

9. $\frac{4}{5} = 0.8$

10. $\frac{2}{7} = 0.286$

11. $\frac{3}{5} = 0.6$

12. $\frac{3}{6} = 0.5$

13. $\frac{3}{4} = 0.75$

14. $\frac{5}{6} = 0.833$

15. $\frac{9}{10} = 0.9$

16. $\frac{11}{20} = 0.55$

17. $\frac{1}{6} = 0.167$

18. $\frac{7}{8} = 0.875$

CD-104321 • © Carson-Dellosa

83

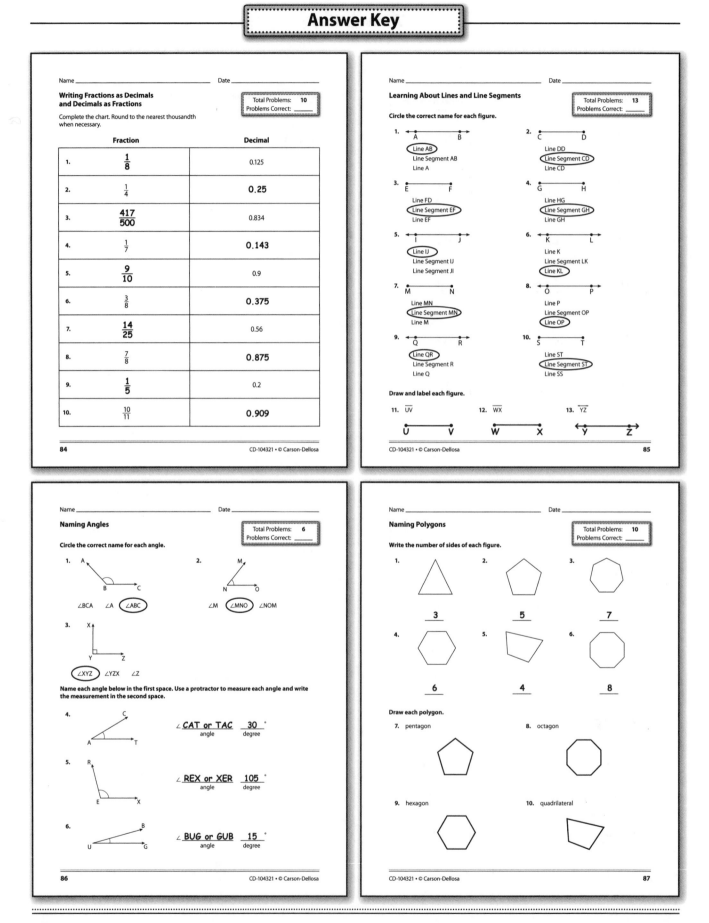

Name _____ Date _____

Writing Fractions as Decimals and Decimals as Fractions

Total Problems: 10
Problems Correct: _____

Complete the chart. Round to the nearest thousandth when necessary.

	Fraction	Decimal
1.	$\frac{1}{8}$	0.125
2.	$\frac{1}{4}$	**0.25**
3.	$\frac{417}{500}$	0.834
4.	$\frac{1}{7}$	**0.143**
5.	$\frac{9}{10}$	0.9
6.	$\frac{3}{8}$	**0.375**
7.	$\frac{14}{25}$	0.56
8.	$\frac{7}{8}$	**0.875**
9.	$\frac{1}{5}$	0.2
10.	$\frac{10}{11}$	**0.909**

84   CD-104321 • © Carson-Dellosa

Name _____ Date _____

Learning About Lines and Line Segments

Total Problems: 13
Problems Correct: _____

Circle the correct name for each figure.

1. ⟨Line AB⟩
    Line Segment AB
    Line A

2. Line DD
    ⟨Line Segment CD⟩
    Line CD

3. Line FD
    ⟨Line Segment EF⟩
    Line EF

4. Line HG
    ⟨Line Segment GH⟩
    Line GH

5. ⟨Line IJ⟩
    Line Segment IJ
    Line Segment JI

6. Line K
    Line Segment LK
    ⟨Line KL⟩

7. Line MN
    ⟨Line Segment MN⟩
    Line M

8. Line P
    Line Segment OP
    ⟨Line OP⟩

9. ⟨Line QR⟩
    Line Segment R
    Line Q

10. Line ST
    ⟨Line Segment ST⟩
    Line SS

Draw and label each figure.

11. $\overline{UV}$ 12. $\overline{WX}$ 13. $\overleftrightarrow{YZ}$

CD-104321 • © Carson-Dellosa   85

Name _____ Date _____

Naming Angles

Total Problems: 6
Problems Correct: _____

Circle the correct name for each angle.

1. ∠BCA   ∠A   ⟨∠ABC⟩

2. ∠M   ⟨∠MNO⟩   ∠NOM

3. ⟨∠XYZ⟩   ∠YZX   ∠Z

Name each angle below in the first space. Use a protractor to measure each angle and write the measurement in the second space.

4. ∠ **CAT or TAC**   **30** °
          angle   degree

5. ∠ **REX or XER**   **105** °
          angle   degree

6. ∠ **BUG or GUB**   **15** °
          angle   degree

86   CD-104321 • © Carson-Dellosa

Name _____ Date _____

Naming Polygons

Total Problems: 10
Problems Correct: _____

Write the number of sides of each figure.

1. **3**

2. **5**

3. **7**

4. **6**

5. **4**

6. **8**

Draw each polygon.

7. pentagon

8. octagon

9. hexagon

10. quadrilateral

CD-104321 • © Carson-Dellosa   87

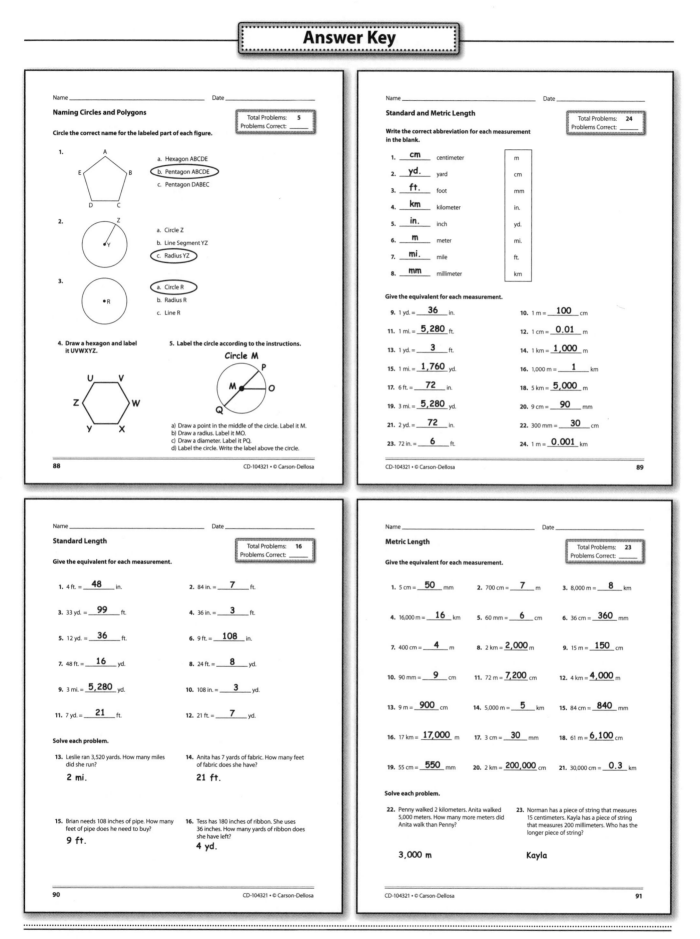

Name _____ **Date** _____

Naming Circles and Polygons

Total Problems: **5**
Problems Correct: _____

Circle the correct name for the labeled part of each figure.

1.
   a. Hexagon ABCDE
   b. (Pentagon ABCDE)
   c. Pentagon DABEC

2.
   a. Circle Z
   b. Line Segment YZ
   c. (Radius YZ)

3.
   a. (Circle R)
   b. Radius R
   c. Line R

4. Draw a hexagon and label it UVWXYZ.

5. Label the circle according to the instructions.

Circle M

a) Draw a point in the middle of the circle. Label it M.
b) Draw a radius. Label it MO.
c) Draw a diameter. Label it PQ.
d) Label the circle. Write the label above the circle.

88   CD-104321 • © Carson-Dellosa

Name _____ **Date** _____

Standard and Metric Length

Total Problems: **24**
Problems Correct: _____

Write the correct abbreviation for each measurement in the blank.

1. **cm** centimeter
2. **yd.** yard
3. **ft.** foot
4. **km** kilometer
5. **in.** inch
6. **m** meter
7. **mi.** mile
8. **mm** millimeter

| m |
| cm |
| mm |
| in. |
| yd. |
| mi. |
| ft. |
| km |

Give the equivalent for each measurement.

9. 1 yd. = **36** in.
10. 1 m = **100** cm
11. 1 mi. = **5,280** ft.
12. 1 cm = **0.01** m
13. 1 yd. = **3** ft.
14. 1 km = **1,000** m
15. 1 mi. = **1,760** yd.
16. 1,000 m = **1** km
17. 6 ft. = **72** in.
18. 5 km = **5,000** m
19. 3 mi. = **5,280** yd.
20. 9 cm = **90** mm
21. 2 yd. = **72** in.
22. 300 mm = **30** cm
23. 72 in. = **6** ft.
24. 1 m = **0.001** km

CD-104321 • © Carson-Dellosa   89

Name _____ **Date** _____

Standard Length

Total Problems: **16**
Problems Correct: _____

Give the equivalent for each measurement.

1. 4 ft. = **48** in.
2. 84 in. = **7** ft.
3. 33 yd. = **99** ft.
4. 36 in. = **3** ft.
5. 12 yd. = **36** ft.
6. 9 ft. = **108** in.
7. 48 ft. = **16** yd.
8. 24 ft. = **8** yd.
9. 3 mi. = **5,280** yd.
10. 108 in. = **3** yd.
11. 7 yd. = **21** ft.
12. 21 ft. = **7** yd.

Solve each problem.

13. Leslie ran 3,520 yards. How many miles did she run?

2 mi.

14. Anita has 7 yards of fabric. How many feet of fabric does she have?

21 ft.

15. Brian needs 108 inches of pipe. How many feet of pipe does he need to buy?

9 ft.

16. Tess has 180 inches of ribbon. She uses 36 inches. How many yards of ribbon does she have left?

4 yd.

90   CD-104321 • © Carson-Dellosa

Name _____ **Date** _____

Metric Length

Total Problems: **23**
Problems Correct: _____

Give the equivalent for each measurement.

1. 5 cm = **50** mm
2. 700 cm = **7** m
3. 8,000 m = **8** km
4. 16,000 m = **16** km
5. 60 mm = **6** cm
6. 36 cm = **360** mm
7. 400 cm = **4** m
8. 2 km = **2,000** m
9. 15 m = **150** cm
10. 90 mm = **9** cm
11. 72 m = **7,200** cm
12. 4 km = **4,000** m
13. 9 m = **900** cm
14. 5,000 m = **5** km
15. 84 cm = **840** mm
16. 17 km = **17,000** m
17. 3 cm = **30** mm
18. 61 m = **6,100** cm
19. 55 cm = **550** mm
20. 2 km = **200,000** cm
21. 30,000 cm = **0.3** km

Solve each problem.

22. Penny walked 2 kilometers. Anita walked 5,000 meters. How many more meters did Anita walk than Penny?

3,000 m

23. Norman has a piece of string that measures 15 centimeters. Kayla has a piece of string that measures 200 millimeters. Who has the longer piece of string?

Kayla

CD-104321 • © Carson-Dellosa   91

Name _____ Date _____

Standard Capacity

Total Problems: **17**
Problems Correct: _____

Give the equivalent for each measurement.

1. 2 tbsp. = **6** tsp.   2. 12 c. = **6** pt.   3. 3 gal. = **24** pt.

4. 2 pt. = **4** c.   5. 5 tbsp. = **15** tsp.   6. 8 qt. = **16** pt.

7. 9 tbsp. = **27** tsp.   8. 14 pt. = **7** qt.   9. 7 pt. = **14** c.

10. 10 qt. = **20** pt.   11. 8 qt. = **2** gal.   12. 12 pt. = **6** qt.

13. 14 pt. = **28** c.   14. 3 tbsp. = **9** tsp.   15. 24 c. = **12** pt.

Solve each problem.

16. If Lindsay has 2 gallons of milk, how many pints does she have?

16 pt.

17. Jeff is making orange juice. If he has 8 quarts, how many 1-cup servings can he pour?

32 servings

Name _____ Date _____

Metric Capacity

Total Problems: **16**
Problems Correct: _____

Give the equivalent for each measurement.

1. 8 L = **8,000** mL   2. 5,000 mL = **5** L   3. 15 L = **15,000** mL

4. 48,000 mL = **48** L   5. 0.4 L = **400** mL   6. 33,000 mL = **33** L

7. 92 L = **92,000** mL   8. 2.1 L = **2,100** mL   9. 7,000 mL = **7** L

10. 6 L = **6,000** mL   11. 800 mL = **0.8** L   12. 27 L = **27,000** mL

Solve each problem.

13. William measures 18,000 milliliters of milk. How many liters does he measure?

18 L

14. Karen drinks 0.5 liter of soft drink. How many milliliters does she drink?

500 mL

15. Mark pours 14 liters of juice at the party. How many milliliters of juice does he pour?

14,000 mL

16. Isabelle buys fifteen 2-liter bottles of soft drink for the party. Her guests drink 18,000 milliliters. How many liters of soft drink does Isabelle have left?

12 L

Name _____ Date _____

Standard Mass

Total Problems: **19**
Problems Correct: _____

Give the equivalent for each measurement.

1. 4 lb. = **64** oz.   2. 1 lb. 25 oz. = **41** oz.   3. 64 oz. = **4** lb.

4. 1,200 oz. = **75** lb.   5. 96,000 oz. = **3** tn.   6. 6,000 lb. = **3** tn.

7. 22 lb. = **352** oz.   8. 4.5 lb. = **72** oz.   9. 32 oz. = **2** lb.

10. 96 oz. = **6** lb.   11. 144 oz. = **9** lb.   12. 160 oz. = **10** lb.

13. 2 tn. = **64,000** oz.   14. 3 lb. 4 oz. = **52** oz.   15. 3.5 tn. = **7,000** lb.

Solve each problem.

16. A produce truck that carries apples and oranges weighs 4 tons. How much does the truck weigh in pounds?

8,000 lb.

17. Vera's game weighs $\frac{1}{2}$ pound. How many ounces does her game weigh?

8 oz.

18. Jan's recipe calls for 1 pound of sugar. How many total ounces does she need?

16 oz.

19. Meredith lifts two 5-pound weights every day. How many total ounces does she lift?

160 oz.

Name _____ Date _____

Metric Mass

Total Problems: **19**
Problems Correct: _____

Give the equivalent for each measurement.

1. 3 g = **3,000** mg   2. 8,000 mg = **8** g   3. 14,000 g = **14** kg

4. 84,000 g = **84** kg   5. 9 g = **9,000** mg   6. 650,000 mg = **0.65** kg

7. 73 g = **73,000** mg   8. 0.8 kg = **800,000** mg   9. 25,000 g = **25** kg

10. 7,000 g = **7** kg   11. 12 g = **12,000** mg   12. 118,000 g = **118** kg

13. 6,000 g = **6** kg   14. 2,000 mg = **2** g   15. 65 g = **65,000** mg

Solve each problem.

16. Megan uses 4,000 milligrams of sugar in her recipe. How many grams of sugar does she use?

4 g

17. Harry measures 15 grams of salt. How many milligrams does he measure?

15,000 mg

18. Jake's book weighs 2 kilograms. How many grams does his book weigh?

2,000 g

19. Peter's recipe calls for 16,000 milligrams of cocoa. How many grams of cocoa does Peter need?

16 g

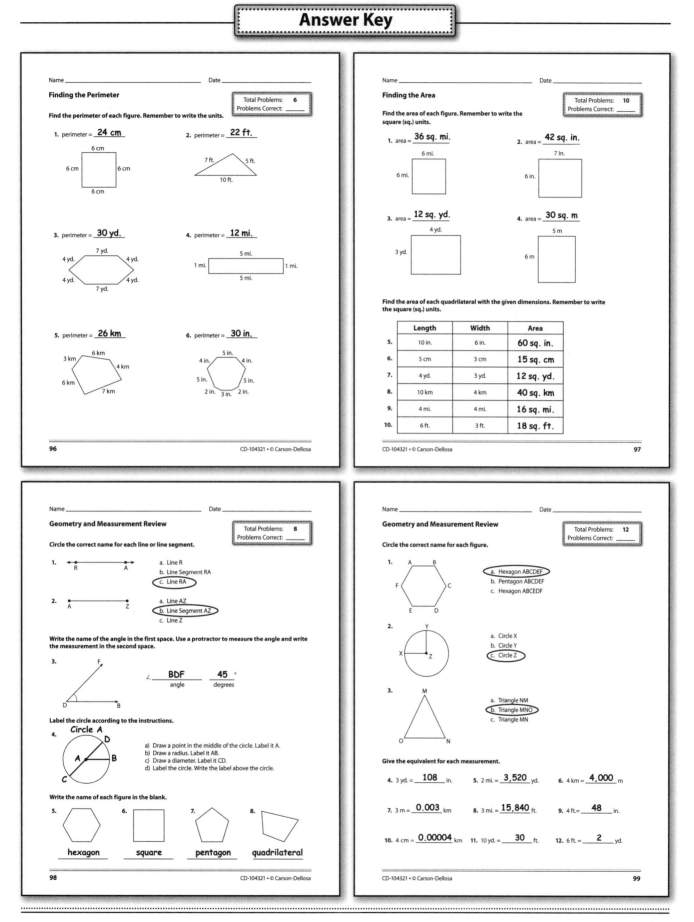

Name _____ Date _____

Finding the Perimeter

| Total Problems: | 6 |
| Problems Correct: _____ | |

Find the perimeter of each figure. Remember to write the units.

1. perimeter = **24 cm**
6 cm
6 cm · 6 cm
6 cm

2. perimeter = **22 ft.**
7 ft. · 5 ft.
10 ft.

3. perimeter = **30 yd.**
7 yd.
4 yd. · 4 yd.
4 yd. · 4 yd.
7 yd.

4. perimeter = **12 mi.**
5 mi.
1 mi. · 1 mi.
5 mi.

5. perimeter = **26 km**
6 km
3 km · 4 km
6 km
7 km

6. perimeter = **30 in.**
5 in.
4 in. · 4 in.
5 in. · 5 in.
2 in. · 3 in. · 2 in.

96   CD-104321 • © Carson-Dellosa

Name _____ Date _____

Finding the Area

| Total Problems: | 10 |
| Problems Correct: _____ | |

Find the area of each figure. Remember to write the square (sq.) units.

1. area = **36 sq. mi.**
6 mi.
6 mi.

2. area = **42 sq. in.**
7 in.
6 in.

3. area = **12 sq. yd.**
4 yd.
3 yd.

4. area = **30 sq. m**
5 m
6 m

Find the area of each quadrilateral with the given dimensions. Remember to write the square (sq.) units.

	Length	Width	Area
5.	10 in.	6 in.	60 sq. in.
6.	5 cm	3 cm	15 sq. cm
7.	4 yd.	3 yd.	12 sq. yd.
8.	10 km	4 km	40 sq. km
9.	4 mi.	4 mi.	16 sq. mi.
10.	6 ft.	3 ft.	18 sq. ft.

CD-104321 • © Carson-Dellosa   97

Name _____ Date _____

Geometry and Measurement Review

| Total Problems: | 8 |
| Problems Correct: _____ | |

Circle the correct name for each line or line segment.

1. R •———• A
   a. Line R
   b. Line Segment RA
   c. Line RA ⟵

2. A •———• Z
   a. Line AZ
   b. Line Segment AZ ⟵
   c. Line Z

Write the name of the angle in the first space. Use a protractor to measure the angle and write the measurement in the second space.

3. ∠ **BDF**   **45** °
    angle   degrees

Label the circle according to the instructions.

4. Circle A
   a) Draw a point in the middle of the circle. Label it A.
   b) Draw a radius. Label it AB.
   c) Draw a diameter. Label it CD.
   d) Label the circle. Write the label above the circle.

Write the name of each figure in the blank.

5. **hexagon**
6. **square**
7. **pentagon**
8. **quadrilateral**

98   CD-104321 • © Carson-Dellosa

Name _____ Date _____

Geometry and Measurement Review

| Total Problems: | 12 |
| Problems Correct: _____ | |

Circle the correct name for each figure.

1.   a. Hexagon ABCDEF ⟵
   b. Pentagon ABCDEF
   c. Hexagon ABCEDF

2.   a. Circle X
   b. Circle Y
   c. Circle Z ⟵

3.   a. Triangle NM
   b. Triangle MNO ⟵
   c. Triangle MN

Give the equivalent for each measurement.

4. 3 yd. = **108** in.
5. 2 mi. = **3,520** yd.
6. 4 km = **4,000** m

7. 3 m = **0.003** km
8. 3 mi. = **15,840** ft.
9. 4 ft.= **48** in.

10. 4 cm = **0.00004** km
11. 10 yd. = **30** ft.
12. 6 ft. = **2** yd.

CD-104321 • © Carson-Dellosa   99

Page 100

Name _____ Date _____

Cumulative Review

Total Problems: **32**
Problems Correct: _____

Solve each problem. Regroup when necessary.

1. 27 +52 = **79**
2. 325 415 +75 = **815**
3. 89 +74 = **163**
4. 7,254 −5,132 = **2,122**
5. 125 +367 = **492**

6. 4,015 3,922 +1,647 = **9,584**
7. 452 −49 = **403**
8. 6,025 4,098 +2,362 = **12,485**
9. 865 −72 = **793**
10. 5,094 −2,678 = **2,416**

11. 92 ×8 = **736**
12. 13 ×63 = **819**
13. 785 ×102 = **80,070**
14. 14)555 = **39 r9**
15. 37)6,721 = **181 r24**

16. 63 × 52 = **3,276**
17. 85 × 919 = **78,115**
18. 362 ÷ 12 = **30 r2**

Write each fraction in simplest form.

19. $\frac{20}{30}$ = **$\frac{2}{3}$**
20. $\frac{24}{48}$ = **$\frac{1}{2}$**
21. $\frac{25}{75}$ = **$\frac{1}{3}$**
22. $\frac{10}{12}$ = **$\frac{5}{6}$**
23. $\frac{35}{140}$ = **$\frac{1}{4}$**

Write each improper fraction as a mixed number.

24. $\frac{8}{6}$ = **$1\frac{1}{3}$**
25. $\frac{25}{10}$ = **$2\frac{1}{2}$**
26. $\frac{51}{15}$ = **$3\frac{2}{5}$**
27. $\frac{16}{9}$ = **$1\frac{7}{9}$**
28. $\frac{120}{18}$ = **$6\frac{2}{3}$**

Write each mixed number as an improper fraction.

29. $1\frac{2}{5}$ = **$\frac{7}{5}$**
30. $4\frac{3}{8}$ = **$\frac{35}{8}$**
31. $3\frac{2}{3}$ = **$\frac{11}{3}$**
32. $7\frac{5}{6}$ = **$\frac{47}{6}$**

Page 101

Name _____ Date _____

Cumulative Review

Total Problems: **28**
Problems Correct: _____

Write the missing numerator to make each pair equivalent.

1. $\frac{1}{3} = \frac{\mathbf{6}}{18}$
2. $\frac{6}{7} = \frac{\mathbf{36}}{42}$
3. $\frac{9}{10} = \frac{\mathbf{45}}{50}$
4. $\frac{3}{4} = \frac{\mathbf{15}}{20}$
5. $\frac{3}{5} = \frac{\mathbf{15}}{25}$

Solve each problem. Write the answer in simplest form.

6. $\frac{3}{7} + \frac{2}{7} =$ **$\frac{5}{7}$**
7. $\frac{1}{4} + \frac{4}{5} =$ **$1\frac{1}{20}$**
8. $\frac{6}{6} - \frac{3}{3} =$ **0**
9. $\frac{15}{17} + \frac{16}{17} =$ **$1\frac{14}{17}$**

10. $4\frac{1}{4} - 2\frac{3}{4} =$ **$1\frac{1}{2}$**
11. $3\frac{3}{9} + 4\frac{5}{18} =$ **$7\frac{11}{18}$**
12. $2\frac{2}{5} + 3\frac{3}{15} =$ **$5\frac{3}{5}$**

Solve each problem. Write the answer in simplest form.

13. $\frac{5}{7} \times \frac{2}{7} =$ **$\frac{10}{49}$**
14. $2 \times \frac{1}{3} =$ **$\frac{2}{3}$**
15. $\frac{5}{8} \times \frac{3}{8} =$ **$\frac{15}{64}$**
16. $\frac{1}{2} \times \frac{4}{5} =$ **$\frac{2}{5}$**

17. $4\frac{1}{4} \times 2\frac{3}{4} =$ **$11\frac{11}{16}$**
18. $2\frac{7}{8} \times 6\frac{2}{3} =$ **$19\frac{1}{6}$**
19. $2\frac{3}{5} \times 5\frac{1}{2} =$ **$14\frac{3}{10}$**

Solve each problem. Regroup when necessary.

20. 3.1 +6.2 = **9.3**
21. 5.9 +4.2 = **10.1**
22. 74.06 −3.1 = **70.96**
23. 86.29 +0.03 = **86.32**
24. 406.34 −26.12 = **380.22**

25. 42.5 + 1.8 = **44.3**
26. 13.1 + 5.5 = **18.6**
27. 34.23 + 16.5 = **50.73**
28. 45.31 − 17.2 = **28.11**

Page 102

Name _____ Date _____

Cumulative Review

Total Problems: **21**
Problems Correct: _____

Solve each problem.

1. 12 ×3.4 = **40.8**
2. 23 ×0.16 = **3.68**
3. 9.63 ×12.2 = **117.486**

4. 0.953 × 0.7 = **0.6671**
5. 0.75 × 0.3 = **0.225**
6. 5)18.5 = **3.7**

7. 0.27)224.1 = **830**
8. 8)25.6 = **3.2**
9. 16)89.6 = **5.6**

10. 121 × 1.2 = **145.2**
11. 89.6 ÷ 16 = **5.6**
12. 0.75 × 3 = **2.25**

13. 0.996 ÷ 12 = **0.083**
14. 0.721 ÷ 7 = **0.103**
15. 0.50 ÷ 2 = **0.25**

16. 2.84 × 16.5 = **46.86**
17. 25.6 ÷ 8 = **3.2**
18. 0.4 × 0.86 = **0.344**

19. 30 ÷ 0.25 = **120**
20. 10 ÷ 0.20 = **50**
21. 70 ÷ 0.35 = **200**

Page 103

Name _____ Date _____

Cumulative Review

Total Problems: **19**
Problems Correct: _____

Write each decimal as a fraction in simplest form.

1. 5.2 = **$5\frac{1}{5}$**
2. 0.5 = **$\frac{1}{2}$**
3. 6.8 = **$6\frac{4}{5}$**
4. 2.52 = **$2\frac{27}{50}$**
5. 12.36 = **$12\frac{9}{25}$**

Write each fraction or mixed number as a decimal.

6. $\frac{1}{8}$ = **0.125**
7. $\frac{3}{4}$ = **0.75**
8. $2\frac{3}{8}$ = **2.375**
9. $5\frac{3}{4}$ = **5.75**
10. $3\frac{3}{5}$ = **3.6**

Draw and label the following.

11. Line QR
12. Line Segment AB
13. Angle MNO
14. Circle S with Radius ST
15. Hexagon HIJKLM
16. Triangle PQR

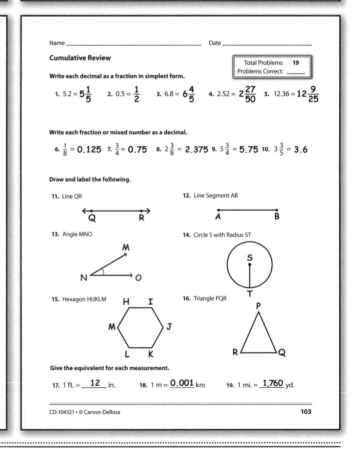

Give the equivalent for each measurement.

17. 1 ft. = **12** in.
18. 1 m = **0.001** km
19. 1 mi. = **1,760** yd.

Congratulations!

receives this award for

Signed

Date

$$6{,}388 + 5{,}122$$

$$51 - 9$$

$$9 \times 6$$

$$142 \times 4$$

$$4{,}990 + 642$$

$$5{,}632 + 62 + 53 + 487$$

$$7 \times 8$$

$$28 \times 3$$

$$25 + 32$$

$$152 + 455 + 111$$

$$7{,}963 - 5{,}741$$

$$18 \times 5$$

$$15 + 8$$

$$8 + 5 + 1$$

$$562 - 14$$

$$12 \times 8$$

11,510	5,632	57	23
42	6,234	718	14
54	56	2,222	548
568	84	90	96

Change to a mixed number in simplest form.

$$\frac{45}{10}$$

© CD

Change to a mixed number in simplest form.

$$\frac{64}{14}$$

© CD

Change to a mixed number in simplest form.

$$\frac{17}{2}$$

© CD

Change to a mixed number in simplest form.

$$\frac{55}{3}$$

© CD

Change to an improper fraction.

$$7\frac{3}{4}$$

© CD

Change to an improper fraction.

$$12\frac{1}{2}$$

© CD

Find the equivalent.

$$\frac{2}{5} = \frac{}{25}$$

© CD

Find the equivalent.

$$\frac{7}{8} = \frac{}{64}$$

© CD

$$\frac{3}{5} \times \frac{2}{9} =$$

© CD

$$\frac{1}{6} \times \frac{7}{8} =$$

© CD

$$8 \times \frac{1}{7} =$$

© CD

$$2 \times \frac{2}{5} =$$

© CD

$$8 \times \frac{1}{10} =$$

© CD

$$3 \times \frac{2}{7} =$$

© CD

$$8 \times 9\frac{1}{2} =$$

© CD

$$2 \times 4\frac{7}{9} =$$

© CD

$18\frac{1}{3}$	$8\frac{1}{2}$	$4\frac{4}{7}$	$4\frac{1}{2}$
56	10	$\frac{25}{2}$	$\frac{31}{4}$
$\frac{4}{5}$	$1\frac{1}{7}$	$\frac{7}{48}$	$\frac{2}{15}$
$9\frac{5}{9}$	76	$\frac{6}{7}$	$\frac{4}{5}$

$$236 \times 419$$

$$615 \times 10$$

$$42 \times 13$$

$$2{,}586 \times 3$$

$$2\overline{)15}$$

$$9\overline{)108}$$

$$8\overline{)48}$$

$$6\overline{)24}$$

$$32\overline{)148}$$

$$15\overline{)75}$$

$$5\overline{)2{,}145}$$

$$4\overline{)124}$$

Fill in the circle with <, >, or =.

$$\frac{10}{12} \bigcirc \frac{9}{13}$$

Fill in the circle with <, >, or =.

$$\frac{2}{5} \bigcirc \frac{4}{7}$$

Fill in the circle with <, >, or =.

$$\frac{15}{45} \bigcirc \frac{5}{15}$$

Change to simplest form.

$$\frac{7}{21}$$

98,884   6,150   546   7,758

7 r1   12 $\underline{6}$ 4

4 r20   5   429   31

>   <   = $\frac{1}{3}$

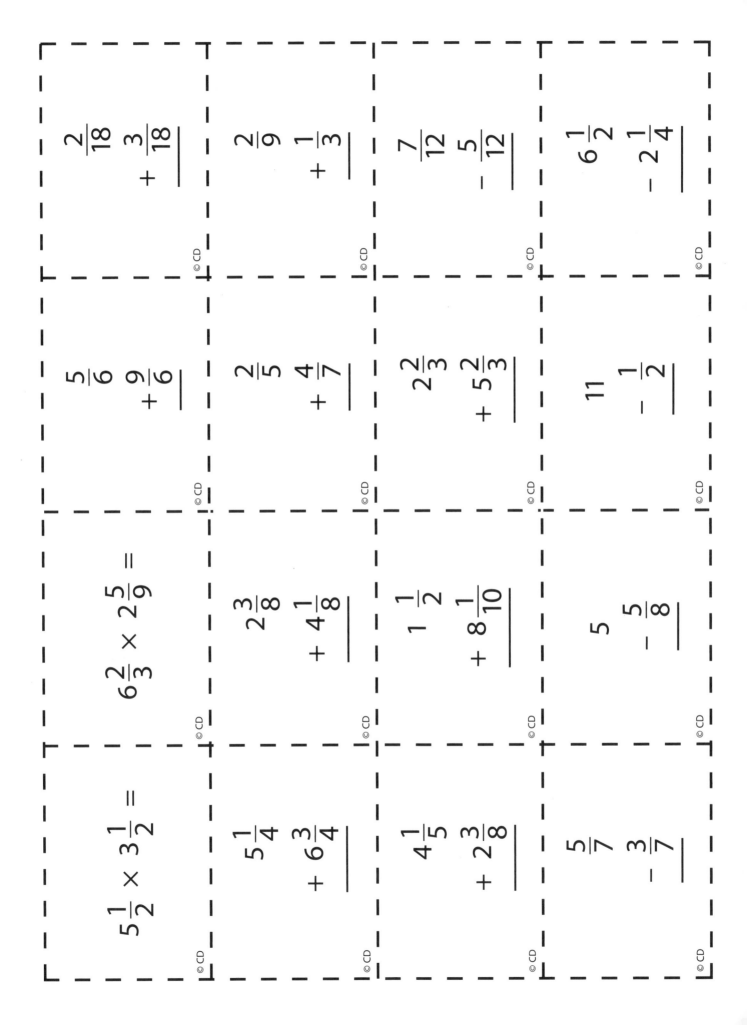

$$\frac{2}{18} + \frac{3}{18}$$

$$\frac{2}{9} + \frac{1}{3}$$

$$\frac{7}{12} - \frac{5}{12}$$

$$6\frac{1}{2} - 2\frac{1}{4}$$

$$\frac{5}{6} + \frac{9}{6}$$

$$\frac{2}{5} + \frac{4}{7}$$

$$2\frac{2}{3} + 5\frac{2}{3}$$

$$11 - 1\frac{1}{2}$$

$$6\frac{2}{3} \times 2\frac{5}{9} =$$

$$2\frac{3}{8} + 4\frac{1}{8}$$

$$1\frac{1}{2} + 8\frac{1}{10}$$

$$5 - \frac{5}{8}$$

$$5\frac{1}{2} \times 3\frac{1}{2} =$$

$$5\frac{1}{4} + 6\frac{3}{4}$$

$$4\frac{1}{5} + 2\frac{3}{8}$$

$$\frac{5}{7} - \frac{3}{7}$$

© CD

$\dfrac{5}{18}$ $2\dfrac{1}{3}$ $17\dfrac{1}{27}$ $19\dfrac{1}{4}$

$\dfrac{5}{9}$ $\dfrac{34}{35}$ $6\dfrac{1}{2}$ 12

$\dfrac{1}{6}$ $8\dfrac{1}{3}$ $9\dfrac{3}{5}$ $6\dfrac{23}{40}$

$4\dfrac{1}{4}$ $10\dfrac{1}{2}$ $4\dfrac{3}{8}$ $\dfrac{2}{7}$

$$2\tfrac{2}{3} - 2\tfrac{1}{3}$$

$$12.3 - 1.5$$

$$11.111 - 2.2$$

$$14.3 \times 8.63$$

$$\tfrac{3}{4} - \tfrac{1}{5}$$

$$16.2 + 44.3$$

$$96.32 - 2.05$$

$$53.3 \times 5.2$$

$$\tfrac{13}{15} - \tfrac{2}{3}$$

$$15.2 + 2.8$$

$$46.9 - 18.3$$

$$0.12 \times 0.04$$

$$4\tfrac{1}{3} - 2\tfrac{3}{8}$$

$$4\tfrac{7}{10} - 1\tfrac{4}{5}$$

$$36.5 - 5.4$$

$$10.2 \times 3.6$$

$$\frac{1}{3} \qquad \frac{11}{20} \qquad \frac{1}{5} \qquad 1\frac{23}{24}$$

$$10.8 \qquad 60.5 \qquad 18 \qquad 2\frac{9}{10}$$

$$8.911 \qquad 94.27 \qquad 28.6 \qquad 31.1$$

$$123.409 \qquad 277.16 \qquad 0.0048 \qquad 36.72$$

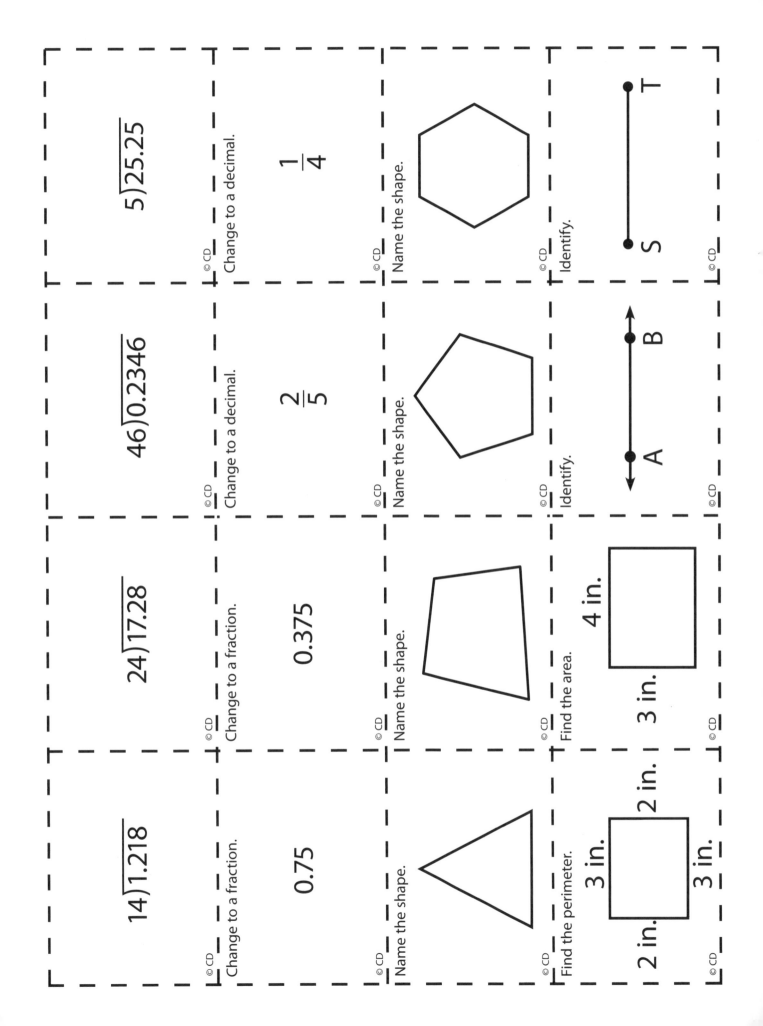

$5\overline{)25.25}$

$46\overline{)0.2346}$

$24\overline{)17.28}$

$14\overline{)1.218}$

© CD

Change to a decimal.

$\dfrac{1}{4}$

Change to a decimal.

$\dfrac{2}{5}$

Change to a fraction.

0.375

Change to a fraction.

0.75

© CD

Name the shape.

Name the shape.

Name the shape.

Name the shape.

© CD

Identify.

S • —— • T

Identify.

A • ←——— B • →

Find the area.

4 in.

3 in.

Find the perimeter.

3 in.

2 in.

2 in.

3 in.

© CD

5.05   0.0051   0.72   0.087

0.25   0.4 $\dfrac{3}{8}$ $\dfrac{3}{4}$

hexagon   pentagon   quadrilateral   triangle

Line
Segment ST   Line AB   12 sq. in.   10 in.